RIDIN' THE WIND

RIDIN' THE WIND

Peter L. Adamski

iUniverse, Inc.
Bloomington

Ridin' the wind

iUniverse books may be ordered through booksellers or by contacting:

iUniverse
1663 Liberty Drive
Bloomington, IN 47403
www.iuniverse.com
1-800-Authors (1-800-288-4677)

ISBN: 978-1-4620-6108-2 (sc)
ISBN: 978-1-4620-6109-9 (ebk)

Printed in the United States of America

iUniverse rev. date: 12/30/2011

Contents

The Wall

Last spring was the first time we were able to visit the wall. My husband and I had long agonized over going to Washington. We knew it would be a very moving and sad experience for both of us. However, we both knew we would one day stand before the wall. We were compelled to. Our only son has his name inscribed in it.

On a warm and beautiful Memorial Day we touched Robert's name. I felt comforted by the fact that Robert is surrounded by the men he had served with. Robert had always wanted to be a soldier. He enlisted at 17, just out of high school. My husband and I had to sign the enlistment papers; he was too young to join by himself. At 18 he went to Vietnam. "I'm in a good company," he had written us shortly after he arrived over there. That was in November. For Christmas we sent him a fruitcake and a book. Robert loved to read. He never got the package. He was killed the day we mailed it.

As my husband and I stood before the wall, the silence of the afternoon was broken with a roar. It was a sound like no other that I had ever heard. Then in the street an endless procession of motorcycles rolled by. Large American flags flew in the breeze and people on the sidewalks cheered. A young woman told us that this was Rolling Thunder. "America's motorcyclists remembering the dead and missing from the Vietnam War." We watched, almost in awe. So many motorcyclists, so many people remembering our Robert and his friends.

As we watched a memory from long ago came to mind. It was of Robert on his 17th birthday. During the party we gave him, he went to the neighbor's house and bought a small motorcycle. It cost him his life's savings, but he didn't mind. Robert rode that little red bike for the year before he left to go in the army.

Had Robert not been killed he'd be in his mid fifties today. A little over weight and thinning on top, just like his father. He'd probably be married and have a family. Though I can only speculate on that, one thing is certain. He would have been here today. Robert was proud of being a soldier, proud that he was in Vietnam.

I looked into every face of every veteran riding pass us. And I looked close. Though I know it's impossible, a little voice tells me Robert is out there in that roaring parade. And soon he'll come riding by, proudly carrying an American flag, spot me, wave and call, "Hi ma!"

Heavenly Ride

Joe had been dead five years when I ran into him on a street corner in New York City. "What the . . ." I exclaimed in disbelief as the tall biker sidled up besides me. He was smiling ear to ear. "Relax. Today is my day," he said in his calming voice.

"But you're dead." I stammered.

Joe looked at me, nodding his head. "Okay, I'm dead. Nobody is perfect. Does that have to spoil such a beautiful day?" he asked with a hurt expression on his face.

I didn't know what to say or do. The surrealness of the situation was freaking me out. Here I was talking with a guy I helped bury. Me and a hundred other guys rode our bikes in his funeral procession. And me and a hundred other guys got drunker than skunks at Joe's favorite bar. All in memory of a stand up guy, a guy who died five years ago.

"You're not Joe," I said defiantly, praying that he wasn't.

"Yes I am," he stated. It was the answer I dreaded to hear.

I was stumped, but I wasn't giving up. "A lot of guys look alike. If you're Joe then prove it to me." I challenged him.

He didn't hesitate. "Remember that ride we took to Boston with those two crazy college girls?" he asked.

"Yeah," I replied. "I can't remember the name of the girl I was with but your girl was Denise. She was a crazy broad." I paused for a second as an elderly woman bumped into me. "Sorry," she said as she turned to me. I continued. "We were both riding our brand new red sporties back then."

He nodded. "That's the ride. And remember on our way home we got caught in that rain storm? The four of us sat under an overpass. We were hunkered down under that filthy bridge and to pass the time you and I talked about rides we wanted to take. And remember the two girls were sitting by themselves crying and cursing us. They were miserable. You went on and on about riding cross country to Washington and then riding the coast highway to LA. Right?"

"Yeah sure I remember that. So what?" I stated forcefully, "I told a lot of guys about making that ride one day."

He stood silent. But only for a moment.

"Well, then picture this," he began. "Two o'clock in the morning. I'm sound asleep. You're wide awake and banging on my door like a mad man. 'Let me in Joe! Hurry up!' you're hollering loud enough for the whole neighborhood to hear."

I smiled as I recalled that crazy night. He continued.

"I let you in and you're higher than a kite. 'Here,' you say as you throw me a wet gym bag. It was crammed full of hundred dollar bills. You said you found the bag next to a dumpster when you went to take a leak behind a bar down at the shore. We figured the money was from a drug deal that went sour. For the next couple of weeks neither one of us went anywhere. We even ditched work. Every time a strange car rode past our houses we about crapped. Man, we were scared."

We both laughed at that long ago experience. "Now," continued the story teller, "I never told anyone about the money. Did you?" he asked.

"Hell no!" I quickly replied.

Joe looked at me and smiled with a calmness I had never seen before.

"It's you! It's really you! Joe, it's really you!" We hugged each other. "Man this is crazy."

Joe and I began slowly walking up town. We hadn't gone very far when I stopped. I had to ask Joe what was on my mind. It was the 800 pound gorilla in the room. "What's it like being dead?" I blurted out.

Joe ran his hands through his long blond hair. "It's like sleeping," he said with a grin. "Nothing much happens till your day comes around."

I was stumped. "What do you mean, your day comes around?"

"We get one day a year back on earth. My day is today, July eighth."

I mulled over Joe's answer. "Sorta like a once a year pass?" I asked.

Joe nodded in agreement. Yes, very much like one."

"Why did you come to the city?" I asked. "Why didn't you go home and visit your family?"

Joe paused, again ran his hands through his long blond hair. "Pete," he said facing me, "could you imagine Donna and the kids seeing me? Or my folks? It'd kill them. Anyway Donna is happy with her new husband and the kids are warming up to Fred. So, I figured I'd spend my day in the Big Apple."

Satisfied, for the moment at least, Joe and I continued our walk. It didn't take long before things started feeling like old times. We grabbed a slice of pizza and a soda, checked out some fine looking ladies and talked about rides we had taken together. Joe had me laughing my ass off when he told me a story I had long forgotten. And I had Joe almost in tears recounting a date I had with my latest girlfriend. However, as much as I tried the 800 pound gorilla couldn't be ignored.

"Do you have to go back?" I asked as we waited for the light to change on Madison Avenue.

Joe laughed. "We all do," he stated.

"What do you mean by that?"

Joe gestured to the crowd of people around us. "Check out the people who look odd or out of place."

"Yeah. So what?" I answered as I surveyed the crowd. "This is New York City, everyone looks odd or out of place."

Again Joe laughed. "Well, look at the guy over there," he said as he pointed to a midget eating a pickle, smoking a cigar and wearing ear muffs. "A little odd to be wearing ear muffs on a 90 degree day."

I had to agree as a grin crossed my face.

"Or look at those two," Joe said. Walking towards us were two grossly over weight middle aged lesbians dressed in matching go-go boots, mini skirts and halter tops. When they passed us Joe remarked "they're almost enough to kill me."

Joe didn't pause. "See him?"

I turned and saw the oddest of them all. Standing at the bus stop was a tall bowling pin shaped man with jet black hair standing on one leg and reciting poetry in German. What was so freaky about him was the fact that he was wearing a Star of David around his neck and swastika arm bands.

A shiver ran down my spine as I was visibly shaken.

"Don't let them bother you, they can't hurt you," Joe reassured me in his calming voice. Then he added, "They'll all be gone tomorrow. Replaced by a new group of equally dead people. New York City is still the favorite city to spend your day in."

I was stunned. "Are you sure they're all dead?" I asked in amazement.

"Not a heart beat in the bunch," Joe casually countered.

We continued our walk.

"Know what I'd like," Joe asked as we stood in line for an Italian ice.

I shook my head. "What?"

"I'd like a ride on a Harley. You still ride one don't you?"

"Hell yes," I snapped as I reached into my jeans' pocket. "This could start one," I said dangling a key in my hand. Joe looked at me like a ten year old at the presents under the Christmas tree.

"You got it here in the city?" He asked.

I smiled. "Yup. It's in a garage a couple of blocks from here." We stepped out of line and started walking cross town at a fast pace.

"Looks good," Joe remarked as he slowly studied the black super glide. "What year is it?"

"It's a 2007," I stated then quickly added, "The dealer gave me a good deal on it."

Joe nodded then squatted in front of the air breather. "Ninety six inches," he read aloud. "I thought the new twin cams were 88 inches."

"The first twin cams were 88 inches. In '07 Harley punched them out to 96 inches."

Joe stood up. "How does it run?"

"Runs great," I answered proudly.

Nonchalantly, Joe threw a leg over the seat. "Well let's run it then," he said.

"Anywhere in particular you want to go?" I asked as I took my seat.

Joe thought for a moment. "Yeah, there is a place I'd like to see again."

"Where's that?" I asked.

"I've always liked the Delaware Water Gap," my erstwhile riding partner remarked.

I pressed the start button. The big twin rumbled to life. "The Water Gap it is." I brought in the clutch lever and tapped the shifter arm.

The ride to the George Washington Bridge was made in typical mid-town traffic. Bumper to bumper, steamy and chaotic. "Some things never change," Joe acknowledged. I nodded in agreement. I was on an adrenalin high. Eager and excited. Eager to get out of the city and excited about taking my good, albeit dead friend for a great ride.

Back in Jersey we got on route 80. Traffic was light and it was moving. It's a straight shot to the Gap, 60 miles distant. I rolled open the throttle and the twin cam pulled. Pulled hard. The speedometer needle rushed past 70, then 80. I kept the throttled opened and the needle continued to climb. The black FXD flew through Hackensack and continued west. "This thing flies," Joe shouted. "It sure does," I said to myself as the needle blasted past 115. The needle had just buried itself when Joe nudged my shoulder.

"Pete," he began, "there's something I have to tell you."

Wanting to hear what Joe had to say I closed the throttle. The big twin slowed down. "Yeah Joe?" I yelled over the noise of the Harley.

Joe leaned forward. "I couldn't let anyone see me on earth. They would have caused a scene. Do you understand?"

"Sure," I answered as I concentrated on driving in what had suddenly become heavy traffic.

"I knew we would meet on that corner this afternoon. It was planned. Sorry man, but Pete it's your time to join me."

I barely had time to ask 'what?' when a Toyota truck swerved into my lane.

February 28th isn't my favorite day. A dusty cowboy town in the middle of Arizona isn't my favorite place. But seniority is seniority and I am low man on the totem pole. I go when and where I am told.

A lone figure on a Harley pulls out of the town's one gas station. The weather beaten gray beard turns in my direction. I stick out my thumb. The biker slows down. Looks me over. Stops. I walk to the idling electra glide.

"Where you going?" he asks.

"Garden Grove, California," I tell him.

He mulls over my answer. "I'm not going that far, but I'll get you a little closer. Hop on." He tells me as he gestures to the back seat.

Just as I was about to throw a leg over the seat he turns. And grabs me by the collar.

Studying my face he sneers, "You look familiar. Real familiar."

"Really? Who do you think I am?" I ask with a smile.

The biker shakes his head, spits on the tarmac. "You look like Pete, a guy I rode with a couple of times back in Jersey."

Again he shakes his head, spits. "You couldn't be him," he states forcefully.

Feigning interest I ask "why not."

"Because," he snaps angrily, "Pete got killed last July when some punk kid in a Toyota truck creamed him."

Georgia Melt Down

T he weather was miserable. Hot, hazy and humid. A real melt down of a day. I tried staying cool by staying in the wind. It worked, that is until my low rider went on reserve. Then it was back into the sauna of a July day in Georgia. I exited the interstate and pulled into the first gas station. While filling up the shovelhead I realized I could use some filling up myself. Fortunately, directly across the street was an establishment that looked like it could quench my thirst. A half a dozen Harley's parked out front gave the joint the seal of approval.

I was rolling through the parking lot when the front door of the bar flew open. A tall, lanky blonde in cowgirl boots and jeans ran down the stairs. She hadn't gone far when a heavyset guy barged through the door behind her. He took two steps, then out of breath stopped. "You better keep running!" He hollered after the fleeing girl. The blonde turned. "Screw you! You fat pig!" She called back. To add emphasis to her words she gave the guy the finger. The guy returned the gesture, shook his head in disgust, spat in her direction. Then he wiped the sweat from his brow, turned and went back inside. I had just come to a stop when the long legged lady walked past. "Are you okay?" I inquired. Without breaking stride she turned to me. "Drop dead." She commanded. Feisty broad I thought to myself. She stomped out of the parking lot and I figured also out of my life. I was wrong.

There was something about the bar that didn't set right with me. It wasn't the other patrons. Most were bikers and no one gave me even a second look as I took a seat at the bar. They were too busy laughing and drinking to pay any attention to a newcomer. And the bar itself was pretty decent. The AC worked, the beer was cold and the jukebox was blaring out 'whipping post.' Any other hot afternoon I'd be able to spend hours there. Hell, I could live there. Not today though. Today I was picking up some very bad vibes. My little inner voice was screaming at me. 'You need to be elsewhere. And pronto." I put a five under my half finished beer and left.

Things hadn't changed in the short time I had been inside. The sun was still out in full force. The humidity was still too high. I was still thirsty. And to top it all off I was now hungry. As I strapped on my brain bucket I asked myself if getting out of there had been the right thing to do. Then I thought back to the last time I had a premonition. About a month ago I was getting on my scooter at a convenience store when some guy walked up to me and started talking about bikes. He went on and on about his chopper. "It's one righteous panhead super glide with ape hangers a mile high." He explained with great relish. The guy was strange enough to give Charlie Manson the creeps. Inside my head alarms are going off. 'This guy is weird. Get out of here!' Before I can gracefully leave two cop cars screech to a stop inches from me. From both cars men in blue jump out, guns drawn. They're yelling and screaming for the guy to get on the ground. Seems not 10 minutes earlier he had murdered his ex-wife and her new husband. Then he casually strolled over to the local 7-11 for a pack of butts and a conversation with me. And the best part was he still had the gun on him when he was arrested.

I got on my scooter and for a second considered kicking the 80-inch shovelhead to life. A bead of sweat rolled down my nose, the starter button would do just fine. A moment later the big twin rumbled to life and I pointed the Goodyear to the street. It felt good to be moving again. I was just starting to cool off when I caught a red light. Immediately after I put my feet to the pavement I spotted her, the blonde with attitude. She was across the street by a phone booth in front of an abandoned used car lot. The light turned green. For a split second I debated whether I should pass her by or stop and try once again to be the Good Samaritan. Against my better judgment I decided to give it the old college try. I stopped in front of the phone booth and instantly regretted my decision. The lady in denim took one look at me, turned and continued on her way down the highway.

It could have ended there. Perhaps should have. But I wouldn't let it. My inner voice was talking to me again. 'Don't let her get away.' It told me in no uncertain terms. I shut off the engine, lifted the helmets visor. "I'm not going to ask if everything is okay." I called after her. "I remember what that got me last time. So how about this? You look like you can use some help. Is there anything I can do?" When I finished I was shouting.

She stopped, turned. Looked me over. "You're not with them are you?" She asked. I shook my head. "No. I'm not with them." That seemed to satisfy her. She drew a deep breath. Slowly let it out, walked towards me. When she got a few feet from me she stopped. "Then I guess I owe you an apology." She stated. "Apology accepted." I assured her. "My name's Gary." I said extending my hand. "I'm Cindy." She answered with a smile. "Hello Cindy." I replied. We shook hands. "I don't know about you, but I'd like to get out of this heat. Maybe get something to eat. Would you like to join me?" I asked. Cindy smiled. "Yes. I'd like that." She quickly answered. I gestured to the back of my bike. Cindy adroitly threw a leg over the seat.

A short distance down the road we found a diner. Despite it being almost noon we were the only customers. "They must have great food." I joked as the elderly waitress led us to a corner table. "This okay with you?" She asked as she handed us menus. "This is fine." Cindy replied. We took our seats. "Do you want anything to drink?" asked the matronly woman. "I can probably drink a gallon of iced tea." Cindy commented. "Ditto for me. And a burger with fries." I added. The waitress wrote on her pad. "Two iced teas and a hamburger with fries." She repeated without looking up. "Make that two hamburgers with fries." Cindy stated. More scribbling on the pad. "Anything else?" Asked the waitress. Both Cindy and I signaled no. The woman left.

We stayed in that diner long after finishing our meal. We sat and talked. We talked about everything under the sun. The more we talked the more we found in common. We enjoyed the same music, exercising and baseball. Cindy was also into bikes. "Especially Harley's." She emphasized. "What else is there?" I asked. Like me, Cindy was a transplanted Yankee. "After graduating from college with a degree in nursing I bid a fond farewell to Michigan and the snow and cold." That was this past January. Now in the middle of a Georgia summer she was starting to regret her decision. "Many a time I've considered moving back." She confessed then quickly asked what brought me to Georgia. "The army." I answered. "I'm stationed at Fort Gordon."

Then I had a question for her. "How did you get mixed up with that crowd at the bar?" I wondered. Cindy rolled her pretty green eyes in disbelief. "A unit coordinator at the hospital set us up. She knew I liked bikes and she knew her nephew rode one. The fact that he was an illiterate slob never entered her mind. And I guess I was too trusting." She paused, sipped her iced tea. When she continued she seemed to be relating a story she had read about. Not one she had lived. "We spoke twice on the phone. Not for very long either time. He was, you might say, a man of few words. However, what little he did say did not endear him to me. He kept asking me to describe how I looked. What I was wearing. Questions a junior high boy would ask. I should have hung up on him. Instead I merely laughed it off." Cindy took another sip of her drink. "Against my better judgment I agreed to go out with him."

"It was a disaster from the moment he knocked on the door." She continued. "Bob lives less than ten miles from my apartment yet he showed up half an hour late. And when he did he had his friends with him. They were a very scary group. They looked like ghouls. Either rail thin or grossly overweight. Long, dirty, unkempt hair. Yellow teeth. You saw them. A couple of them had the high quality tattoos one gets in prison. Just the kind of men I have been searching for all these years. The only thing missing was the word loser written across their foreheads. The whole bunch of them eyed me like lions looking at a lamb. You talk about the hair on the back of your neck standing up." Cindy shuddered. "Why I ever got on his bike is beyond me."

"The ride was nice. The country we passed through was beautiful. This was the first time I had been on a bike since last summer and it felt oh so good. I was even beginning to think things might turn out well after all. Then we stopped at the bar. That's where things got out of hand. He crowded me into a booth. No sooner had I got seated then he started pawing me. Trying to keep cool I joked with him. 'Down boy.' He just grinned. Then he and his friends started drinking. It's only a little after eleven and they're going at it like there would be no tomorrow. I tried talking with him. Wasted energy. He was too busy being stupid to talk. What little he did say was barely above babble. And of course he was pressing ever closer to me. If this isn't a nightmare I don't know what is. Then he started talking to me. Dirty talk. I'm scared. Real scared. Before I was just disgusted. I had to get out of there. So I told him I had to go to the ladies room. I did have to go. He let me pass, watched me every step of the way. No sooner did I sit down on the toilet then he casually walks in on me. I pulled up my pants and ran like hell."

When we left the diner the day was even more miserable than when we had entered it. "Don't you just love the deep south?" Cindy remarked with sarcasm. I took the helmet off the sissy bar and handed it to her. "Are you sure you don't want to wear it?" She asked. "No doubt whatsoever." I told her. The thought of strapping a helmet on my head had never been more unappealing. Cindy paused for a moment, looked at the helmet in her hands. "Then I won't wear it either." I secured the unwanted helmet to the sissy bar.

It was just shy of 80 miles to Cindy's apartment. And though we were on the road for close to two hours and we traveled both interstate and city roads we never saw a cop. Hence I didn't get a ticket for riding without a helmet. "Not one cop! I wouldn't have believed it if I didn't just do it." I stated in near disbelief as we got off the bike. "Two weeks ago my buddy Charles let me take his new sportster for a spin. I was going to ride around the block so I didn't put on a helmet. I didn't make it to the end of the street before a cop pulled me over. And now to ride as far as we did without either of us wearing a helmet is," I paused, searching for the right word. The blonde gave me one of her killer smiles. "You got the Midas touch." She laughed. For a moment I looked at her and all I could think was how lucky I was to meet her. "Yeah." I finally remarked. "I think I have the Midas touch." We walked to her apartment.

The following morning Cindy and I rode to the local IHOP for breakfast. Then it was back to her apartment where we spent much of the day by the pool. While Cindy thumbed through fashion magazines I read a mystery novel I found in the laundry room. A couple of times we jumped into the water and splashed about. We couldn't do much more as there were too many people in the pool.

Cooled off and refreshed we'd return to our reading. For lunch we joined the couple in the next apartment for a BBQ. Then it was back to the pool. All in all it was a very relaxing way to while away yet another miserable summer's day in the peach state. In fact it was about the least exciting day I could imagine. However, I certainly wasn't complaining. All I had to do was turn my head. Not two feet from me was a beautiful woman stretched out in a bikini that gave new meaning to the word skimpy.

I sensed their presence the moment they entered the pool area. It was Bob and one of his friends. I tapped Cindy on the shoulder. "Company." I said gesturing to the uninvited guests. Cindy took a quick look, put her magazine down. In a flash she was out of her chair. "What are you doing here?" She demanded in a voice loud enough for everyone to hear. The two men stopped. "Well look it here," Bob stated to his partner as his eyes took in every inch of the scantly clad Cindy. "She's a beauty all right now isn't she Ron?" He said with obvious glee in his voice. Ron nodded his head in agreement. "That she is." He whistled. Bob started to say something, however, Cindy cut him short. "You're not welcomed here. Now leave." Bob feigned being hurt. Then he laughed. "Well if that isn't the most ungrateful thing you ever heard I don't know what is. All we is doing is checking up on you. Making sure you got home in one piece." He explained with a grin. "She got home in one piece." I interjected. Then added. "Why don't you guys just leave?" Bob turned to me with a sneer. "I was talking to her." He stated forcefully. Before I could answer Cindy snapped. "And I told you to get out of here. If you don't leave I'll call the police." It didn't sound like a threat. It sounded like a course of action she was ready to take. The two men held their ground in silence. Both men had looks of nonplus on their faces. "They did not know what to do or say. However, they didn't have long to think things over. "Well," Cindy asked in a voice one would use to talk to a misbehaving child or a dimwitted adult. "Get moving." The two men meekly looked at each other. Then they turned and walked away. Cindy and I watched till they disappeared from sight. "Remind me never to get you mad at me." I said with a laugh. Cindy looked at me, put her arms around my waist. "Thanks for being there. I couldn't have done it without you." She remarked wistfully.

Cindy and I started spending every free moment together. After duty I'd shower, change into jeans and jump on my low rider. Half an hour later I'd be knocking on her door. Some nights we'd go out for dinner, other nights she'd cook for us. On Friday nights I'd bring enough clothes for the weekend. A couple of times she came onto post and we'd catch a movie or exercise in the gym. I taught her to play racket ball and quickly learned that not only was Cindy attractive and intelligent she was also very athletic. By the end of the month there was no doubt as to how we felt about the other. We had fallen in love.

The memory of Bob and friends had all but faded into oblivion the Saturday morning we set out on a weekend run. We couldn't have asked for a better day. Temperatures were only in the upper 70's, above us the sky was a robin egg blue and for once there was an absence of humidity. It was a perfect day for a bike ride. And ride we did. The Harley carried us effortlessly mile after mile. Life couldn't be better than this, I thought to myself.

The campground was swarming with bikes, people and tents. There were people laughing, dogs barking, bikes rumbling. It was great. We rode slowly as we searched for a spot to pitch our tent. When we passed a group of bikers getting settled Cindy tapped my shoulder. "Over there." She said pointing across the field to a small opening in the tree line. "Looks perfect for one bike." She remarked. "Should give us some privacy." I turned the handlebars to where Cindy had pointed.

After putting up the tent we walked through the campgrounds. We stopped often to talk with people or to check out the bikes. When the air came alive with music we sat down under a tree at the top of a small knoll. We couldn't see the band, however, that didn't matter. We certainly could hear them and they were pretty good. When they played the opening riffs to 'gimme three steps' Cindy started swaying to the music. Then she wrapped her arms around my neck and gave me one hell of a kiss. "I love you." She softly whispered in my ear.

Under that tree we were oblivious to everything and everyone around us. However, our reverie was short lived. "Hey, isn't that Cindy?" A guy called. "Yeah. "That's the bitch." Came a second mans voice. Cindy and I watched as Bob and another guy started towards us. They stopped a few feet from where we sat. "Hey Cindy, you gonna walk home from here too?" asked Bob's companion. This brought a laugh from both men. I got to my feet, sized the two men up. Bob was big, probably 250 or better. Fortunately, most of it was fat. His partner was just the opposite. He couldn't have weighed more than one twenty. Neither appeared to have showered in days. Dressed in ratty clothes they looked like extras from a sixties B biker movie. Almost laughable. Still two against one is not good odds. I knew if there was a fight I'd have to end it quickly. We stood eyeing each other in absolute silence. Even the band had stopped playing.

Bob broke the silence. "Hey buddy, there ain't nothing between you and me." The big man stated forcefully. "My beef's with the bitch." He spat his words. I looked him straight in the face. "Why don't you and your friend just keep moving?" I said in a calm, deliberate voice. He gave me a good once over. For a moment he looked like he was going to take a swing at me. Then he thought better of it. Instead of throwing a punch he took a long drink of beer and belched. His friend roared with laughter. Bob turned to his sidekick. Another belch, more laughter. Then he focused his attention back on me. "You're the guy at the apartment." He stated. Or asked. "Yes I am." I shot back. Again he sized me up. He spit on the ground, then jabbed his big paw in Cindy's direction. "Now I got a beef with her and you." He sternly warned me. Silence. "We'll meet again." He advised me. "Till then," I fired back. The two intruders continued on their way.

"I'm glad you didn't fight." Cindy said the moment I sat down. "That makes two of us." I told her truthfully. I had definite plans for the night and those plans did not include answering a lot of questions asked by cops or doctors. Cindy snuggled close; the band resumed playing and life in this little corner of the world returned to a more peaceful bent.

Sunday's weather was a carbon copy of Saturday's. Another beautiful day. And like the day before Cindy and I had a good time. But like all good things the day had to end. The ride to Cindy's apartment went all too quickly. It seemed that one minute we were packing our saddlebags and the next minute we were pulling into her driveway. "I can't believe how fast the weekend went." Cindy remarked as we got off the bike. I nodded in agreement. A few minutes later I was making that lonely ride back to Fort Gordon.

The following Friday night Cindy and I rode to Jacks, a somewhat dark and dingy tavern a few miles out of town. Cindy had taken me there once before. It was in her words, 'a fun cheap date.' What the place lacks in class it makes up with great bar food, a first class jukebox and two pool tables. Though Jack's wasn't a biker hangout occasionally individual riders or clubs would stop in. They'd have a beer, shoot a game of pool. The regulars were mostly middle-aged guys having a beer or two after work.

There were about half a dozen customers when we walked in. Off in a corner booth were three patch holders and their women. They were quietly drinking beer and talking amongst their little group. Cindy made a beeline for the pool table while I ordered a couple of bar pizza's and two glasses of beer. My eager competitor starting racking the balls. "Straight." She called to me. "Fine with me." I fired back as the barkeep slid over the glasses of liquid gold. "To the game of straight and my favorite person in this whole crazy world." I said as she took a glass. "To us." She pronounced. Our glasses clicked. "Now down to serious stuff." Cindy said as she put her glass on a table. "You break. And may the better woman win." Soon the bar was filled with the sound of ivory balls crashing into each other.

Cindy beat me handily the first two games. "You forget how to play?" She teased. "No, I didn't forget. It's just that I got a funny feeling." I replied in almost a whisper. Cindy paused. Then she came over to me, put her arms around my neck. "You okay?" She asked. I nodded. "I'm fine." I told her as I wrapped my arms around her tiny waist. I pulled her body close to mine. Kissed her neck. "I like this." Cindy whispered. "But do you think this is the right place for that?" She asked with a mischievous grin. I started to answer, but paused. I didn't want to talk over the rumble coming from the parking lot. A group of Harley's had just pulled in and their riders were revving their engines. When the last motor was shut off I continued. "My inner voice says we should go."

Cindy grabbed our helmets and we started to leave. Before we took two steps the door opened and the bikers began coming in. The first guy headed straight to the men's room. Seconds later another biker entered. He called to his friend. "That'll teach you to eat a whole pizza." He let out a hearty laugh as the first biker let out a curse. The bathroom door was locked. Cindy and I looked at each other and smiled. However, our smiles didn't last long. The third biker thru the door was all too familiar to us.

My main squeeze stopped in her tracks. "It's Bob." She stated.

The big man took a couple of steps towards the bar. Then he stopped, letting his eyes adjust to the semi darkness. He looked the room over. When his gaze fell on us he grinned. It wasn't a friendly sort of grin. I felt Cindy shiver.

"He won't do anything in here." I assured her. A moment later Bob casually joined his friend at the bar.

As we started for the door I slipped Cindy the keys to the low rider. "When we get outside start the bike and get on it." Cindy nodded.

I opened the door and we stepped into the night. Cindy hurried to the bike while I took a position behind the door. Seconds later the Harley came to life. I began to count to ten, but only got to five before the door flew open. Out charged Bob. He took a step in the direction of the idling Harley then stopped. He was not interested in Cindy.

"You looking for me?" I called.

He turned, a sneer on his face. "Yeah. I'm looking for you." He growled.

"Well here I am. Fat man." I taunted him. He took the bait. The heavyset man lunged at me.

Instinctively I stepped to the side and delivered a roundhouse kick. It hit pay dirt. Bob dropped both hands to his groin. From the expression on his face he was in agony. Before he could recover I kicked him again. This time in the face. He dropped to his knees. Then I kicked him a third and then a fourth time. Bob fell with a thud face first onto the pavement. The fight was over.

I surveyed my handiwork. The big man was a crumpled mass on the sidewalk. "Sensei Jim would be proud." I said half aloud.

The door opened and out stepped the other two bikers. "Damn." I muttered. The biker who had run to the bathroom studded Bob lying on the ground. Then he turned to me. "Fair fight?" He asked. I nodded my answer. The biker shrugged his shoulders.

"Can't ask for more than that." Commented the other biker. The two of them turned and went back inside Jacks.

I walked over to Cindy who was sitting on the Harley's p-pad.

"Let's go back to your place. I'd like to shower."

One of Cindy's killer smiles came over her face. "Mind if I join you in that shower?"

"Not at all."

I threw my leg over the bike.

Full Circle

W e stood motionless as the last light of another summer day sank behind the Arizona mountains. My wife Donna and I were in awe of our surroundings. The incredible beauty of the desert. Golds. Reds. Blues. It was a virtual kaleidoscope of colors. Off in the distance a lone 18-wheeler silently traveled west on the interstate. We watched it until it disappeared from sight. Then as if by magic another truck took its' place. And then another. Yet not a sound could we hear. In this little corner of a very colorful world all was at peace. "Beautiful," I whispered to Donna. The wispy blonde squeezed my hand once, then a second time. It was our silent way of saying yes.

Donna brought her sportster to life. A single beam of light pierced the night. I turned my Yankees hat around, pressed the super glide's starter button. The twin cam powered Harley awakened with a rumble and a second beam of light pierced the night. For a long moment we sat and listened to the big V-twins idling beneath us. Their rhythmic beat was a comforting, familiar sound and feel. With the beauty of the heavens above and the gentle vibrations of a Harley beneath me my mind drifted. Only when Donna revved her engine did I snap out of my reverie. "Ready?" she asked with a smile. I nodded, brought in the clutch, shifted into gear. Two Harley's went slowly into the darkness.

Donna and I rode side by side, barely doing forty. We were the only ones on the state highway. Far to our left a storm raged. Bolts of lightning streaked, illuminating the horizon. They came so fast, one after another, that the desert appeared to be awash in a white liquid. "What a Fourth of July!" Donna called excitedly. She too was enraptured with the beauty of the storm. "All we need," I shouted back, "is for God to play riders on the storm." We both laughed. To us the storm was surreal. We saw it, but felt it not. All we heard was the sound of our motors. We rode on.

We pulled into a dimly lit gas station. Donna's peanut tank was on reserve. "Ninety five miles," she stated as she unscrewed the gas cap. "That's the trouble with this tank," Donna continued as she put the gas nozzle inside it. "Just when you get going you gotta stop." I nodded in agreement. "Great looking tank. Just ain't enough of it." I remarked. Donna finished, handed me the hose. Then she walked to the edge of the parking lot. There she watched the raging storm. It was growing ever more violent. The flashes were quicker, brighter and coming closer. After filling my tank I went to join Donna. Suddenly the entire southern sky was lit up in the most incredible display of nature's powers I have ever witnessed. It was so overwhelming I simply stopped and watched. Then, for the briefest moment of time, I caught sight of Donna. She was stretching, as if reaching to the heavens, her entire body silhouetted in white. With her long blonde hair blowing in the breeze she looked like a Goddess.

An hour later Donna was dead, struck down by a drunk driver. We were but a block from our house when the pick up truck ran the stop sign. The driver was a neighbor. He and his wife were our friends. When he staggered out of the cab I could have killed him. Instead I gently held my Donna and cried.

That was three years ago. I no longer live in Arizona. The company that I work for was kind enough to transfer me to the east coast. They say the pain of losing a spouse never goes away. I believe them. Donna was the woman I had loved since the eighth grade. She was the woman who had loved me with all her being. People said we were 'soul mates,' the 'perfect couple.' Her sister called us 'lovers who are friends.' Not a day goes by that I do not think of Donna.

Life goes on. After a long hiatus, I am again in the wind. The first few rides were hard. I kept looking in my rear view mirror expecting to see Donna on her sportster. Once, while riding on the interstate, my mind drifted. Memories came flooding back. The rides we had been on, the places we had visited, the friends we had met along the road. The love we shared with each other. In no time there was a smile on my face and tears streaming down my cheeks. The Lord knows I loved my Donna!

About a month ago I started dating Barbara. We met in the local Harley dealership. She was buying a T-shirt for a friend's birthday; I was having my bike serviced. The attractive brunette had caught my eye the instant she entered the building. Something inside me said this woman is special. Do not let her get away. I walked up to her and said hello. She smiled and we began to talk. That was the beginning of what appears to be a very good relationship.

Barbara is a nurse. She works the four to midnight shift in the emergency room. This past Saturday we had plans to go for a motorcycle ride after she got off work. It was a few minutes before twelve when I pulled into the hospital's parking lot. It was not until nearly five hours later that Barbara and I would start our ride. "One emergency after another and three nurses out," Barbara explained.

Barbara was exhausted. However, she still wanted to go for a ride. "Are you sure about this?" I asked. "I'll be fine," she insisted. Then quickly added. "I've been telling the other nurses that my boyfriend was taking me on my first Harley ride tonight. Now you're not going to make a liar out of me are you?" She asked with a grin. I returned her smile. "Of course not."

I pressed the super glide's starter button, a single beam of light pierced the night. Moments later the big twin rumbled onto the highway. Then it was as if some force guided me, steering us south. Then for reasons I cannot explain I exited the parkway and rode towards the shore. Then suddenly, Barbara and I were on the boardwalk.

We stood motionless as the first light of another summer day rose above the ocean. Barbara and I were in awe of surroundings. The incredible beauty of the ocean. Golds. Reds. Blues. It was a virtual kaleidoscope of colors. Off in the distance a lone ship slowly passed. We watched it until it disappeared from sight. Then as if by magic another ship took its place. And then another. Yet not a sound could we hear. "Beautiful," I whispered to Barbara. The pretty woman squeezed my hand once, then a second time.

Memories

The black sportster rumbled down Main Street sounding as if it were straining to be set free. When it came abreast of the crowd in front of Tony's Bar & Grill the rider gave a thumbs up. Then he cracked the throttle. The 900 screamed, took off on its' rear wheel. Those watching from the sidewalk cheered as the tricked out 'CH blasted down the street. When the rider reached the intersection of Main and Willow he closed the throttle, put his boot to the pavement and did as smooth a U turn as ever seen on a flat track. Moments later the rider was backing his scooter to the curb in front of Tony's.

The crowd gathered around the smiling rider. Everyone was laughing and joking. A heavyset guy slapped the sportster rider on his back. "Casey you're nuts!" He bellowed. Others called out similar comments. "He's also pretty damned lucky." Another biker remarked pointing down the street. Everyone turned and watched as a cop car pulled out of Willow onto Main.

No two ways about it, Casey was lucky. Perhaps, as the one biker stated, he was damned lucky. Good luck came so natural to Casey that one had to wonder if he did not lead a charmed life. The close calls on his bike, the way women came on to him, the ease with which he went through life. That was fine with Casey; he took it all in stride. Nothing bothered him. When asked the secret of his success he would just shrug his shoulders and mutter 'damned if I know.'

Casey was a biker, pure, plain and simple. He was lean and ragged with tats on both arms. His hair was long and he always was in need of a shave. He had a crooked smile and a chipped front tooth. Casey wore ratty work shirts, grease stained jeans and scuffed combat boots. Dress him up in a tuxedo and put him in the back seat of a Rolls Royce and people would still say 'look at that biker.' The quintessential biker had a devil may care attitude. He lived life to its fullest. "If it's going to happen, it's going to happen so I might as well enjoy it." He once explained to me.

Casey was one of a handful of guys I hung out with a good number of years ago. We weren't a club, though we did on occasion jokingly call ourselves 'the no name gang.' Tony's was our unofficial headquarters. Wednesday night was our unofficial meeting night. Over pizza and beer we would make plans for the upcoming weekend. Some rides would be day trips. Eastern Pa, southern New York. Other rides, like the trips to the Jersey shore would be weekend deals. When we set off on our runs we did so from Tony's.

Tony's had been a biker hangout for years. There always seemed to be a Harley or two lined up in front of the place. Loners and club members alike felt welcomed. Guys shouting back and forth, drag pipes blasting out that great V-twin beat was the background music of Tony's. The sounds of bikes and bikers blended nicely with the aroma of Tony's Italian dishes. Mixed in with the bikers were the women. More than our fair share I would say. Most were local college girls. Eighteen and nineteen year old hard bellies looking for a thrill now that they weren't living under daddy's roof. There was of course, from time to time, the rift raft bikers attract. Call it the biker curse.

George, the owner of Tony's, did not mind us hanging out at his place. Our money was good and we spent it freely. For the most part the other patrons seemed to enjoy our company. The couple of times the cops stopped by it was a more of a social call than official business. Mike's older brother Sean was a sergeant on the force. He would occasionally park his patrol car and shoot the breeze with the guys. He rode a Triumph 650, a fact that got him some good-natured ribbing. Another cop who came around and talked with us was Fred. The first time he saw me he laughed. A few years earlier, he reminded me, I had dated his younger sister. I couldn't remember a thing about the date. The only thing I remembered about her was her huge tits. The other cops were decent guys, too. Everybody was local. Other than the occasional burn out when we left Tony's we never caused any problems. We were just a bunch of guys who liked to ride motorcycles and hang out together.

As I mentioned earlier there were women. George had his Nancy and Steve had his Karen. Both were serious relationships. Willie had just started dating Irene, a college student who looked like she was twelve years old. He caught more than a little crap over her fawn like features. When Irene asked Willie if he could get a date for Linda, her roommate, he immediately thought of his best friend Casey. The night the girls showed up everyone busted a gut laughing. Linda could have been Irene's kid sister! She even had freckles! Casey and Irene were, for obvious reasons, nicknamed the odd couple. Irene and Linda turned out to be terrific people. Dresser Mike did not have a girlfriend. He had girlfriends, lots of them. As George was quick to point out, "one was uglier than the next." Dresser Mike would just smile. "So what? Who cares what they look like when they're hanging on behind me?" He would ask. "And who cares what they look like when the lights are off?" Dresser Mike got his moniker from the bike he rode, a fully loaded seventy-four. Parked among the choppers and sportsters it stood out like the proverbial sore thumb. To the other guys Dresser Mike's FL was 'a garbage wagon.' Dresser Mike just blew off such comments. "It's a class bike." He'd answer his critics.

When I started hanging out at Tony's I wasn't seeing anybody. Like most of the other guys I had spent a couple years away from home courtesy of the United States government. However, I quickly got back into the swing of things and was soon dating Arlene. Arlene was a waitress I met at an all night diner on route 17. She was well built with long raven colored hair. She loved bikes and was always ready to get on my sportster. Arlene was also as smart as a rock. She fit my bill perfectly.

Tony's was the place to spend time with your friends. Especially on a hot summer's night. The AC worked, the beer was cold, the food was decent and the jukebox was filled with great records. One minute you could be inside listening to the Doors and the next you could be outside listening to a stroked shovel being fine-tuned or blown out. Something always seemed to be happening inside Tony's brick walls or on the sidewalk outside its door. There was an air of excitement about the place.

Then there was that biker curse. Drawn to Tony's and the biker scene, like moths to light, were lowlife's, the scum of the earth. Most were harmless. Guys wearing Harley T-shirts and spouting off about the panhead they rode or the sportster they chopped. "It's one righteous bike," they would tell anyone who would listen. Sometimes drunks would panhandle for their next drink. Occasionally a hooker would try to ply her trade amongst the guys. That was almost laughable. With so much free stuff available who would pay for it? Most of our uninvited guests would hang around for a few minutes, say what they had to say and then move on.

However, not all of them went away peacefully. On a Saturday afternoon in late September or early October there was the 'incident.' I was not there; Arlene and I had split the night before for a weekend at a bed & breakfast in Vermont. Casey had been there and the following Monday evening he filled me in on what went down. We were in his garage changing the oil in our bikes. Linda sat on a stool thumbing through a stack of dog-eared motorcycle magazines.

"Did you hear what happened the other day at Tony's?" Linda asked as I rolled my sportster into the garage.

I shook my head. "No. What happened the other day at Tony's?"

Casey remained silent as he slid a brick under my kickstand.

"Tell him what happened!" Linda called out.

The lanky biker paused. Then he told how he and Willie were to meet at Tony's before riding to meet Linda and Irene at their dorm. Casey got to Tony's ten or fifteen minutes early. He was standing on the sidewalk smoking a cigarette when a mustang pulls in next to his bike. "The guy gets out. College kid. He walks up to me. 'You Casey' he asks. The kid says his name is Dave and that he is Linda's boyfriend from high school." Casey paused for a moment.

I let out a whistle. Then solemnly state. "You have to be careful of old high school boyfriends."

My good friend smiled. Then he continued. "It quickly became apparent that Dave did not like bikers. He especially did not like the biker who was doing his old high school sweetheart."

Linda looked up from the magazine she was holding. Casey turned in her direction and then gave her a shit-eating grin. "And doing the young lady twice a day." He let out a laugh. Linda laughed, and then shot back. "Twice a day. In your dreams!"

Casey and I laughed even harder and my friend gave his girl a-thumbs up. "Very nice." He complemented her.

Casey continued telling the story. "The guy kept getting in my face. We were eye ball to eye ball." He related. "Finally, I had enough of this guys crap. I got up in his face. 'You going to do something or are you just going to shoot off your mouth?' I say with the biggest smile possible." Casey paused, waiting for me to ask the inevitable question. Finally I did.

"Well, what the duck happened next?"

"The guy cursed, then went to his car." The lanky biker stopped, placed a drain pan under my XLCH. Then he continued. "Two seconds later he's back and he's got a pistol. He started waving it around, pointing it at me. The guy was ranting and raving, threatening to kill me." Casey stopped, turned to Linda. "What kind of boys did you date in high school?" He asked with mock indignation.

Linda, always quick with the reply, snapped back. "Guys who could do me twice a day. Something I gave up when I started hanging out with bikers."

The three of us busted out laughing.

"Casey, maybe you better just stick with telling the story." I advised my friend as I tried to regain my composure.

"Yes, sweetheart. Why don't you just stick to the story?" Linda seconded in her sweetest voice.

Casey drew a deep breath, and then resumed telling the tale. "To say I was scared would be a gross understatement." Casey confessed. "However, I wasn't going to let some little shithead screw with me. So I blew the biggest smoke ring ever in his face and told the guy if he shot me it would be in my back. I turned and walked away." Casey paused as he readied a can of oil to pour into my bikes' oil tank.

I said the first thing that came to mind. "Holy shit." Then quickly added, "Go on."

"I hadn't taken two steps when a half a dozen cop cars screeched to a stop." Casey continued. "Out jumped a lot of men in blue suits, guns drawn. My friend Dave meekly put his pistol on the sidewalk. Then he was handcuffed and put in a cop car."

For the next couple of weeks the 'incident' was the buzz at Tony's. Anything new or exciting was compared against it. Not many things even came close. The 'incident' became part of the local lore. It also added to the legend of Casey. Here was a guy who when confronted by a whacko with a gun blows a smoke ring in the guys face and walks away. It took a couple of weeks but life at Tony's finally got back to it's regular beat. I guess it goes to show that things weren't too wild back then. After all, what did you expect? We were just a bunch of guys who liked to ride motorcycles and hang out together.

Winter came early that year. Over the Thanksgiving weekend I called it a season and tucked the sportster in the garage. Arlene and I continued to go out until just after the start of the new year. We called it quits, but remained friends. Then in February, sick and tired of the snow and cold I loaded everything I owned in a truck and headed to a sunnier climate. I had intentions of making it to the Golden State. However, at a gas station in Arizona I met Barbara. It was love at first sight and we have been together in Arizona ever since.

I don't get back east too often. Barbara and operate a kennel in Mesa that keeps us pretty busy. However, I did get back to Jersey for a wedding this past spring. The afternoon I was to return home I took a slight detour on my way to the airport. My destination was a brick building on a street filled with memories. After I parked my rent a Ford at the curb I checked out Tony's. I compared it with my memory and was amazed; the place hadn't changed in more than 30 years. The only thing missing was a Harley parked at the curb. I thought of going in, having a slice or two and inquiring about George, but at the last moment changed my mind. Satisfied with my little trip down memory lane, I started the Ford. I was about to put it in reverse when I heard a familiar sound. Seconds later that sound transformed itself into two Harley's, a low rider and a softail, idling in the next parking space. I looked over as the two passengers climbed off. The young ladies walked to the sidewalk, took off their helmets. As their beau's backed their scooters to the curb they shook their long blonde hair loose. A moment later the guy on the low rider revved his engine. The straight piped twin cam sounded good. When he backed off the other guy picked up the slack. His twin cam sounded even better. Then the first guy opened up his mill again. This show of noise brought laughter to the two college age girls.

I smiled as I drove away. Some thing's never change.

Not A Bad Life

K aren's phone call was like a bolt of lightning out of a blue sky. The call was unexpected and most certainly not welcomed. It became evident very quickly that she had been drinking. Knowing Karen, she had been drinking heavily. The pretty blonde rambled on about us getting back together. "Why did we have to break up?" She finally asked. I almost busted out laughing. However, in a very calm voice I told her the reason. "Karen, don't you remember? You dropped me for George." That didn't slow her down. "Well," She continued, "you shouldn't have let me." That was the last thing I heard her say. I put the phone under the other pillow and went back to sleep. It was a few minutes after two and I had to be at school at eight-fifteen.

Later that morning as I graded my second grader's math papers I thought back to when Karen and I dated. It was, to put it succinctly, a crazy time that somehow or another went on for just shy of a year. She was the girl every biker dreams of meeting. Karen was good looking, had a ton of money, liked to party and loved Harley's. She especially loved fast Harley's. My low rider was a screamer and Karen never tired of throwing a leg over it. And to tell you the truth I never tired of her hanging onto me as I banged through the gears. We would spend two or three evenings a week at one bar or another. I don't drink, however I quickly learned that Karen could drink for the two of us. When she was feeling no pain we'd jump on the low rider. For my main squeeze's pleasure I rode that twin cam like a 17 year old on a Ninja. The tach's needle was always buried in the red.

We would scream down back roads and interstates. It didn't matter. Our nights would end at her house or my apartment. I preferred the former; Karen lived in a very nice home less than a mile from the school where I taught. Many a morning I pulled into the teacher's parking lot bleary eyed and half asleep. But also very satisfied.

As I said earlier, Karen had money. Her father owned two very successful car dealerships. No expense was too much for his only child, his princess. He bought her whatever she wanted. She was spoiled beyond belief. Every once in a while Karen would spend a day keeping her father company at the dealership. Karen didn't have to work, and many days she never got out of bed. Either she didn't feel like doing anything or else she was sleeping off a drunk.

On the other hand I had to go to work. I wasn't burdened with student loans and my low rider was mine. However, I had the regular expenses: rent, food, gas. Bills that I had to pay. There was no rich father taking care of me. Karen and I met the day I was hired to teach. We were at 'Snookers', a downtown bar that caters to yuppies. My boss and good buddy Mike took me there to celebrate my new job. "It'll be my treat." He had promised me. "Unless you order something to eat or drink." To tell the truth I have never felt comfortable in a bar. I don't drink or smoke and generally don't hang out with people who do. However, Mike was my best friend from elementary school. After high school he didn't go to college, instead he hired four guys and started a construction company. Mike had the luck of the Irish and his business did very well. During my college days and for the two plus years after graduation that I searched for a teaching job I worked for Mike.

'Snookers' was pretty quiet the night we went there. In spite of his joking Mike bought me a steak dinner. The two of us were sitting at our booth talking when a sassy blonde got up from her table and walked in our direction. Both Mike and I smiled as she passed. "That alone is worth the price of the meal," Mike stated as he watched her go into the ladies room. I nodded in agreement.

I sensed her presences before she spoke. Turning I was pleasantly surprised to see the sassy blonde standing next to me. "Do you ride a Harley or do you just wear the T-shirt?" She asked. "I ride." I answered, then turned back to my meal. Not two seconds passed before she spoke again. "I'd like to go for a ride." She stated. I put my fork down and turned to her. I sized her up, and more than liked what I saw. "I very much would like to take you for a ride; however, my best friend and I are eating now. When we finish you will get your ride." For what seemed an eternity she stood there, not knowing what to say or do. Weeks later she told me that she was stunned. "No guy had ever not agreed to do whatever I wanted, whenever I wanted," she explained. Then without saying a word she went back to her table.

Mike was in a state of shock. "Are you crazy?" He asked.

I shrugged my shoulders. "Maybe I am." I told him. "But, I'm also hungry."

Karen got her ride on my Harley that night. Not knowing that she was a speed addict I didn't open up the 88 inch low rider. That is until she tapped me on my shoulder. We were stopped at a traffic light. "Go right," She called over the rumbling drag pipes, and then quickly added, "get on the interstate." I nodded, the light changed to green, I turned right. The ramp was long and straight, perfect for getting up to speed before entering the super slab. I slowly opened the throttle, letting the power build gradually. I felt Karen's arms tighten their grip on me. Then I heard her scream, 'open this bad boy up!' That was the start. From that night on whenever we went on the bike we'd fly up that on ramp, then blast down I-10 like there wasn't another living soul on the planet.

Karen and I never took long walks, visited museums or went to the movies. We didn't do most everything a normal couple does. The meals we ate together were in bars. Our conversations were never very deep. Mostly recounting the day's events. I cannot ever recall us having a discussion about politics or world events. I never met any of her family or learned much about her private life. Conversely, she never learned much about me.

Our joint history could be summed up quite simply: "They met in a bar, went for a ride on his Harley then had sex. Again and again." That was exactly what I was looking for. I was too young, way too young, to have a serious relationship. And to tell you the truth Karen was the last woman in the world I would want to get serious with. Certainly she was attractive, wealthy, loved Harley's and could party all night. She was also an alcoholic. At times she was stupid beyond belief. Like the night she stood up from her bar stool, turned and puked on the lady sitting next to her. Or the time she tripped over her own two feet and nearly knocked over the waitress. Then there were the times, too numerous to count, where she seemed to try her best to get me into a fight. She would flirt with some guy, getting him all hot and bothered, then snuggle up next to me. Most guys shrugged it off as the antics of a drunk while a few became belligerent. Fortunately, God gave me a silver tongue and I never had to fight.

One night in either late March or early April Mike gave me a call. This was about six months after Karen and I started going out.

"You'll never guess who I bumped into last night?" He teased.

"Since I'll never guess, why don't you just tell me?" I answered.

Mike laughed, then blurted out, "Grace Napoli."

Grace Napoli was a name from out of the past. Grace, Mike and I had grown up in the same neighborhood. It was a tight knit, all American middle-class community. Everyone knew everyone else. Grace was younger than us, by eight or nine years, but we definitely knew each other. I last saw Grace five years ago while visiting my parents. Back then she was tall and as skinny as a rail. We had a nice conversation that spring day. Grace talked a mile a minute, a typical teenager, I remember thinking to myself. She was polite, sweet and thoughtful. All in all Grace was a good kid in my book.

Mike went on to tell me that Grace had moved back to southern California a few weeks ago. "She was living in Arizona with her mom, but came back to be near her father," he explained. Then he quickly added, "She was asking about you."

After Mike and I hung up I phoned Grace. The young lady answered with a friendly, "hello Steve." From that auspicious beginning the conversation only got better. We talked and laughed for more than an hour. She had a keen memory and told stories of the neighborhood I had long forgotten. Grace recounted how once my dog had gotten loose and I chased him through her parents back yard. "You would call him and he'd stop, then when you got near him he would run away. It was so funny," she recounted, "it was like watching a comedy." I thought back to that day and laughed. "Willie listened very well," I explained, "only trouble, he didn't obey."

Grace and I agreed to meet the following evening for dinner. She gave me the name and directions to an Italian restaurant she was partial to. "See you at six."

I pulled into the parking lot a few minutes before six. I had no sooner shut down the low rider then in the next row the door to a late model Pontiac opened. Out stepped a young lady that definitely caught my eye. First of all, she was very attractive. Then there was the clothes she was wearing. Her blue jeans looked like they were spray painted on her long shapely legs. Tucked into her jeans was a blue button down blouse. She wore bright red lipstick and sunglasses dark enough that one could stare at the sun. This young lady was the complete package; she could have been a movie star. Oh yeah, she wore one other thing that got my attention, a beautiful smile.

"Hello Steve," Grace said as she extended her hand.

I was barely able to shake her hand and I know I babbled when I said, "hello Grace."

If Grace was the least bit nervous she never showed it. She was the picture of coolness. Later, over dinner, she coyly asked, "I've changed, haven't I?" "Yes you have," I assured her as I looked deep into her brown eyes, "I don't remember you having such large hands."

I very much enjoyed that evening with Grace. After dinner we walked to a nearby park where we sat on a bench and talked. When we parted we hugged and promised to keep in touch. "You know my telephone number," she called out as she drove off. "I most certainly do," I said as I waved good-bye.

Karen ended our relationship. She gave me the news one morning as I was leaving her house to go to school. "I found someone new," was all she said. No further explanation was needed or given. Karen and I had never talked about a future together. Our relationship was long, but it was of the moment. Ours might have been the emptiest relationship in history, but we were true to the other. Karen was always honest and up front with me. She never went out behind my back, nor did I ever go out with another woman. Not even with Grace. The half dozen or so times Grace and I had gotten together were never dates. We would take a relaxing ride, have a meal together and mostly just talk. Grace was a terrific person and a great friend who just happened to be a very attractive woman.

Grace was out of town the night Karen broke up with me. When she returned home a few days later she gave me a call. Grace was pretty excited about the trip she had just taken. She and a girlfriend had spent a week in Hawaii. "The weather was terrific and the

beaches were beautiful," she gushed. She went on and on about the
hotel, the food, the nightlife. The more Grace talked the more I was
reminded of that spring day so many years ago when Grace and I met
in front of my parent's house. She could talk a mile a minute and the
more she talked the more I realized I liked listening to her. She was
vibrant, alive. She was also funny.

"The second day around noon," Grace recounted, "Connie and I
went for a swim in the hotel's pool. The pool was packed with college
kids. I was wearing a very skimpy bikini. I mean it was tiny! Connie
had dared me to wear it, never believing that I would. Well I did. Let
me tell you, it didn't cover much. I got in the pool. When I was in up
to my waist I closed my eyes and ducked my head in the water. When
I stood up I kept my eyes closed. I stood absolutely still for what
seemed forever. It felt so good, the water running down my face, the
warmth of the sun on my body. When I finally opened my eyes was I
ever surprised. Floating in front of me was my top! Of course every
guy was looking at me. I just smiled, casually picked up the top and
put it on. One guy started cheering. Then another, and another. Soon
all the guys were standing up and whistling and cheering."

I said the first words that came to mind. "I wish I could have
been there."

The phone went silent and I instantly regretted my words. Before
I could apology Grace broke the silence.

"I wish you could have been there too." She stated. Then she
quickly added, "I would have liked that. You being there."

Not twenty minutes later I was knocking on Grace's apartment.
She opened the door wearing her infamous bikini. She was right, it
didn't cover much. It covered even less the second she said, "All I did
was lean over and this happened."

That was a year ago. A lot has changed since that night. Grace
and I most definitely did become more than friends. After what we
laughingly called the bikini episode how could we not? However,
our new relationship did not last but three or four weeks. In that
short time we learned that we had little in common except that we
grew up in the same neighborhood. That alone could not sustain a
relationship. Try as we both did, things did not work out. The end
came on a Thursday night. A few weeks later Mike mentioned that
Grace had moved back to Arizona.

Where does all this leave me? Pretty much where I was at the start of this story. I'm still teaching and I'm still riding. In fact I'm getting ready to walk out the door helmet in hand as I write this. I hadn't planned on going anywhere tonight, but then Karen called. This time I talked to her. The pretty blonde may have slurred her words, but her intent was clear. She misses me and wants me to take her for a motorcycle ride. "Please. It'll be fun," she pleaded. "And after the ride it will be just like old times," she promised. It took me a whole second to make up my mind. "See you in ten minutes." I said with a grin.

Dad's last words

I'm not a religious guy. I don't go to church on Sunday and I don't lead the best of lifestyles. But, I do believe in God. It's just that I can't bring myself to always be asking Him for a favor. That's all praying is, asking God for a favor. I'm sure with all God has to contend with my problems don't even register on his radar screen.

However, tonight I'm asking God for two favors. Please keep the state police busy elsewhere as I shoot up the interstate at speeds well above the posted limit. And, please let me see my father before you take him.

My older sister Irene called a few minutes after nine. I was on the couch watching some inane reality show when the phone rang. I had barely said hello when Irene let loose.

"Dad's real bad. He's in the hospital. If you want to see him you better get here tonight."

Ten minutes later I was shifting my low rider into gear. Before getting on the interstate I pulled into a gas station. Knowing that I'd be burning fuel much faster than normal I squeezed every last drop into the Fat Bob tanks.

As I was leaving the gas station I was joined by a Harley dresser. The rider wore full leathers and a gold painted full faced helmet. We nodded to each other than accelerated up the onramp together. I was surprised that the electra glide could stay with my low rider, but it did.

Once on the interstate and in sixth gear I kept the speedometer needle pegged on eighty five. So did the guy on the dresser. He took up position a few yards behind me and to my right.

The night was cool and traffic was exceptionally light. A full moon lit up the night. It was a perfect night for riding. It was also perfect for doing some inner thinking. And that is what I did.

Dad and I were never close. I don't think we ever played catch or went to a ball game together. Or did any of the other hundreds of things dad's do with their kids.

I'm certain that I'm partially at fault. I was a rebel. I was always getting into trouble. Nothing serious, just typical kids crap. I'd cut school, hang out at the mall, stay out late. I was also a bit loose with the tongue.

Dad didn't take too kindly to having a wiseass for a son. He was a career soldier and the behavior of his family directly reflected on him. Still dad rose through the ranks. He was a first sergeant when I left to live on my own after graduating from high school.

Throughout high school, hell my entire life, two things have held my interest. Bikes and women. I quickly learned that having a Harley was no hindrance to meeting women. Some might even suggest that riding a HD helped.

When I got into bikes dad was pissed. "Do you want to kill yourself?" he snarled at me. He kept this up until one day I had an answer for him. "No, I don't want to kill myself. Do you? You're the one who keeps reenlisting in the infantry." Dad was speechless. "Try riding a bike one day. You'd like it." I shot back.

My first Harley was a sportster. Say what you want about sportsters, but mine was great. It ran and ran despite countless wheelies, panic stops and a complete lack of maintenance. I abused that one thousand from the day the dealer rolled it off the floor to the day I traded it in for a super glide.

My twenties were a blur. I was making good money painting bikes. And I was spending it just as fast. There was always a party, a rally or a blonde to ride away with for a long weekend. And some of my money was just plain wasted.

Fortunately, over the years I calmed down. Today I own a two bay garage and paint shop. 'Just V-Twins' has been good to me. It has allowed me to buy a house and live a decent life.

I've even settled down with one woman. Cindy and I have been living together for two years. She's a nurse I met one night at a gas station. Funny thing, Cindy had never been on a bike till I took her for a ride.

Whereas my life had been going well dad's life took a turn for the worse. Shortly after Irene graduated from college mom split from him. Then dad retired. That was the worst mistake he ever made. Dad loved the army. Without it dad just gave up the will to live.

Dad rented an apartment about 150 miles from me. Irene lives in the same town as dad. They've remained close, for which I am glad. Dad and I talk on the phone about once a month. I've been to his place twice in the seven years he's lived there. He has yet to visit me.

I was lost in thought when suddenly a deer ran across the road just yards in front of me. I grabbed the front brake and stomped on the rear brake pedal. The twin cam's tires screeched as they hauled the bike to a near stop. A massive bolt of adrenaline shot through my body and my heart raced. "Damn, that was close," was all I could say. A moment later I slowly accelerated.

I had just gotten up to speed when I noticed the dresser. Lost in my thoughts I had forgotten about him. However, there he was, a few yards behind me and to my right. He was exactly where he had been when we first got on the interstate. When the rider noticed that I was looking at him he waved. I returned the gesture.

Within a few minutes we were once again making time. It felt great blasting down a near deserted highway at eighty. I slowly opened the throttle, glanced at the speedometer. It felt great blasting down a near deserted highway at ninety. It felt even better blasting down a near deserted highway doing the ton.

That is, until my left mirror lit up blue and red. Instinctively I closed the throttle. I looked over my left shoulder. The cop car was gaining on us. Then in a flash it passed us!

My heart was still racing when a mile down the road I took the exit for the hospital. I parked the bike and trotted across the lot to the emergency room. Seconds later I was entering my father's room.

Irene and her husband Charles were standing next to the bed. Irene was crying as she held dad's hand. Seeing me she smiled. "Look who's here," she whispered into dad's ear.

I bent to my father's side. His breathing was slow and labored. The end was near. Dad turned to me. Then in a voice barely above a whisper he said, "That was some ride wasn't it?" I didn't know what he meant.

Irene leaned forward. "What do you mean pop?" Irene asked.

A feint smile came over dad's face. "We almost got that deer." Then he passed.

When the nurses came into the room Irene, Charles and I stepped into the hallway. There we discussed funeral arrangements and dad's rather bizarre last words.

"It was funny," Irene related, "dad kept talking about almost getting a deer. I wonder what he meant."

"I think," Charles said somewhat hesitatingly, "that your dad was talking about a hunting trip he and I went on a few years back. There was a deer that we tracked but could never get. That's what I think your father meant." Irene nodded and I shrugged my shoulders. "What else could it mean?" I threw out.

It was a few minutes after midnight when we left the hospital. Irene wanted me to spend the night at her house. "You're tired," she said, "and you've got a long ride ahead of you." I thanked her but declined the offer. "Riding always does me good," I answered as I toyed with my keys.

We parted at the entrance to the emergency room. As I walked to my bike I was joined by two cops. Their patrol car was parked next to my bike.

"How's it going officers?" I asked when they came abreast of me.

The cop closest to me turned, yawned then let out a deep breath. It was obvious he was tired. "Same old crap," he stated, "different day."

The other cop, the taller of the two, just chuckled. I nodded my head in agreement. We walked across the lot in silence.

When we reached our vehicles the tired cop followed me to the side next to which my bike was parked.

"Well, good night guys," I remarked as I went to insert the key into the ignition slot. The once sleepy cop had stopped a few feet behind me. Suddenly he was wide awake.

"Tonight's your lucky night," he announced loud enough for his partner to hear. However, I knew he meant the remark for me.

For a moment I was stunned. "Is there something the matter?" I asked with a smile as I turned and faced him.

"It's him," the first cop called to his partner, "the screaming Harley."

The taller of the two cops joined us. Bending down he studied my license plate. "Bingo," he stated, "it's him."

The cop closest to me grinned. "Tonight's your lucky night," he said.

"What do you mean?" I asked perplexed.

The cop smiled. "We got you on radar doing 101."

"Couldn't have been me," I said with almost a straight face. Both cops laughed.

"Good try. About an hour ago you flew pass us going like a bat out of hell. No sooner did we turn on the lights then the call came that we had to respond to an emergency in the hospital."

Again the tired cop yawned. "You're luck because we're too tired to write you a ticket."

I rubbed my jaw. "Guess the night was a wash. No ticket but my father died."

The two cops expressed their condolences.

"I guess the other guy should count his lucky stars too." I casually remarked.

The two cops looked at each other. Then they turned to me.

"What other guy?" They asked.

"The guy riding behind me on the dresser," I answered.

Again the two cops looked at each other. When they turned to me both had blank expressions on their faces. "There was no other bike."

For a long moment the three of us stood there in silence. Then from just outside the door to the emergency room a nurse called my name.

"Yes," I called back.

"We have something of your fathers." She signaled me to join her.

I pocketed the key. "Excuse me gentlemen," I said to the two cops. Seconds later I was opening the emergency room door.

The nurse was quick. "The cleaning room attendant found this in your father's room." She reached to the chair next to her. Then she handed me a gold colored full faced helmet.

Seven Year Itch

I guess there is something to the seven year itch theory. That's about how long my marriage lasted. One morning I woke up in a house on a tree lined street, that night I went to sleep in a one bedroom apartment next to a strip mall.

However, all wasn't lost. I kept my Harley, which I rode a lot after the separation. Some nights after work I get on the sportster and before I knew it we were in front of my old house. Old habits die hard.

I'm lucky in another way too. The ex and I have remained friends. We split because we grew apart. She worked nine to five, Monday through Friday as an office manager and I worked four to midnight, Thursday through Monday as an emergency room nurse. Not exactly a schedule that promotes a happy family life. At first we joked that we slept in the same bed just not at the same time. That quickly got old.

One sultry Friday night in late June I rode the 1200 to the hospital in spite of a 40% chance of showers. Half way through the night that forty per cent became a down pour. "It looks like you're going to get a wet ass," one of the other nurses called as she came in from a cigarette break. Fortunately the rain stopped shortly before my shift ended.

As I am more than a little anal immediately after parking the sporty in the garage I started cleaning it. I had just applied a coat of wax to the front fender when I paused to watch a familiar white

Chevy enter the lot. It pulled into the spot next to my Ranger. When the driver opened the door I started waxing the tear drop gas tank.

Her high heels echoed off the blacktop. When they stopped I looked up. The attractive woman stood just outside the garage.

"Cleaning your motorcycle," Donna commented in her soothing voice.

Besides being anal I have a bit of wise ass in me. I turned suddenly, looked at the bike, the rags in my hands. "Damn!" I stated with mock surprise. "I thought I was cooking dinner." Donna and I both laughed.

I gestured to a chair. The blonde declined. "I've been sitting all day." She explained.

"Would you like to join me?" I asked in jest as I held up the bottle of wax.

Her answer surprised me. "Only if I get to go for a ride," Donna shot back.

"Sounds fair to me," I answered.

Donna hesitated for a moment. Then she blurted out, "I'll be right back, I have to change clothes." I nodded in agreement. I resumed waxing the gas tank to the sound of high heels scurrying across the parking lot.

Her return caught me by surprise. I was squatting facing into the garage cleaning the forks when she announced that she was back. I nearly fell over backwards.

"Sorry for startling you," she laughed. "If I had known that I had snuck up on you I would have popped a balloon." I stood up and grinned. "I see you're a wise ass too."

Donna smiled. Then she reached for the T-shirt in my hand. "I can do that."

We switched places. I picked up the bottle of armor all and began spraying the seat. No sooner had I started to wipe the seat then Donna called to me. She had the T-shirt wrapped around one fork leg. "See," she said as she began stroking the fork leg, "I can do it." When she stopped she licked her lips and smiled. Then she pointed to my crotch and laughed. "You're so easy to get hard." I just smiled. "Let's go for that ride," I said as I extended my hand. Donna took it and together my ex-wife and I walked across the parking lot.

Lucky Thunder

Sometimes it's lucky to be unlucky. Take yesterday for instance. Around eleven I was walking out the door when I paused for a moment. I was going to visit Husein who is in the hospital recovery from surgery. Seems a teenager didn't know that a stop sign means just what it says. Stop. The kid blew right through it and hit the back of Husein's sportster. My long time riding partner was banged up pretty good. Fortunately the doctors say he'll make a full recovery.

As I was saying, I was walking out the door when I paused for a moment. A question ran through my head. "Should I or shouldn't I grab my denim jacket?" Half of my brain said yes. "It's a hot one, you need to keep your exposure to the sun to a minimum." The other half of my brain said no. "What are you nuts? Wear a jacket? It's 90 degrees out. You'll be fine in your T-shirt." The rest of my brain (a little Yogi Berra there) simply said screw it. "Just ride." The denim jacket stayed in the closet.

The ride to the hospital was beautiful. The sun was shinning and traffic out of town and on the interstate was light. To add icing to the cake the super glide's 96 cubic inch engine purred. For most of the seventy-mile ride the speedometer's needle was pegged at eighty. However, there were more than a few instances when it touched ninety and once when it passed the ton. Luck was with me-every cop I saw was busy writing motorists tickets.

Husein was thumbing through a motorcycle magazine when I entered the room. "How's the patient?" I asked as I went over to him. "Getting stronger every day." Came his reply as he put down the magazine. We shook hands then I slumped into a chair by the bed. We shot the bull for more than an hour. Talked about bikes, rides we were going to take (next year) and broads. Seems there was a particular nurse Husein had his eye on. "A real beauty," he told me. Then he gave me the bad news. "She thinks bikes are dangerous." We both laughed.

When I left the hospital I could not help but notice the obvious. The once hot, sunny morning had disappeared. In its place was a cool, dark afternoon. I pressed the start button, put my helmet on. Traffic was heavy on the interstate and I had to keep my eyes on the road. Still I could see the black clouds swirling off in the distance. Not a good sign. Two other not good signs quickly appeared. The first was the fact that every car traveling in the opposite direction had their headlights on. Some even had their wipers going. The second sign was bad news in capital letters. Out of those black swirling clouds bolts of lighting were flashing. Before I could say a nasty word a big fat raindrop exploded on my face shield. Then another one. Then ten thousand more exploded over every inch of my body. To keep my neck from being drilled by the little stingers I pulled my face shield down. My neck was saved, but not my arms. They were exposed and they were hammered. Within seconds I was drenched.

I took the first exit looking for a biker hotel. Immediately off the interstate was a underpass. I got the FXD as close to the curb as possible, then settled in for the duration of the storm. I kept the bike running and the right blinker on. That seemed to work, cars and trucks gave me a wide berth as they passed.

Just as I was thinking things might work out I saw it coming. The biker hotel I was staying in was on a slight incline. Now as every second grader knows, water runs down hill. I could only watch as the brown river flowed over my feet. To make matters worse, it was a wide river. It stretched out nearly to the second lane of traffic. It was also deep, it covered my sneakers. No sooner had I resigned myself to the fact that I was going to stand in ankle deep water then a passing car drenched me. Then another. Before a third car passed I shifted into gear and slowly accelerated.

Just past the overpass was a strip mall. Every strip mall in the world has a pizza joint, I reasoned. I would wait out the storm eating pizza. This strip mall was the exception. No pizza joint. However, it did have a bagel shop. It would have to do. I dripped my way to the counter helmet in hand. The guy behind the counter surveyed me, watched as I tracked up his floor with water. I must have looked like a drowned cat. "It's a nice day." He stated with a friendly smile. I chuckled. "Yeah," I shot back, "if you're a duck." He chuckled then came back with, "it could be worse." He paused for a second then added "You could be riding a motorcycle." I plopped my wet helmet on the counter. "I am riding a motorcycle." I stated in a very matter of fact tone. The heavy-set man's smile disappeared, but only for a second. "It could be worse," he repeated, "You could be a long way from home." I let out a sigh, nodded my head dejectedly. "I am a long way from home." This brought a instant and loud response from the man. "Then what you need my friend is a nice dry shirt!"

"And you have a nice dry shirt?" I inquired.

Now it was his turn to look dejected. "No. I do not. But, if I did, I would gladly sell it to you."

"And if I had," I informed him, "a bridge over the east river named after a borough of New York City I would gladly sell it to you."

With helmet in hand I took my bagel and soda to a table by the window. The rain was coming down steady and rumbles of thunder could be heard. I resigned myself to the fact that I wouldn't be going anywhere soon. How to kill time in a small town? Fortunately, on the next table was a local newspaper. The big news in this part of the world was about a woman who yesterday had robbed her third convenience store in the past two weeks. She always wore shorts. The police dubbed her 'chicken legs.'

I was about to put the paper down when a bolt of lighting struck. It was very loud and very close. Instantly I looked out the window. Stopped just on the other side of the glass was a young lady. She too was looking across the street. Her sixth sense must have told her that she was being watched for suddenly she turned. I smiled, then faked like I was wiping sweat off my face. "Close call." I mouthed.

She smiled and started to walk off.

I tapped the window. She stopped, turned. Again I smiled, then gestured for her to join me.

She paused for a moment. Then she shook her head. She would have taken two steps, but, I was out the door next to her before she could. "According to the guy behind the counter it's a nice day, unless you're riding a motorcycle. And I am riding a motorcycle. And also according to the guy behind the counter things could be worse if you were far from home. And I am far from home. So please don't let a soaking wet bike riding fool who is far from home have even a worse day than what is he already having. Please join me. I'll buy you any bagel your heart desires."

When she finished laughing the pretty brunette smiled. "Never let it be said that I made a wet, miserable biker's day worse then it already is."

As I opened the door for her the guy behind the counter smiled.

Cindy Was Right

Cindy was not a happy woman. She was in her mid thirties, divorced and living from payday to payday. Her job was both physically demanding and dirty. Even worse Cindy was not only estranged from her ex-husband but her 11 year old son as well. In all her years she never pictured herself in such dire circumstances.

Cindy and I worked on the shipping docks of a large distribution center. I didn't mind the hard work, it kept me in shape. And what 21 year old guy doesn't want to keep in shape? And the money wasn't bad, not for a guy living rent free in an apartment his parents owned and going to college under the GI Bill. Whereas Cindy had to work full time just to pay her bills I worked part time to save for my up coming cross country motorcycle ride.

Cindy and I hit it off from the first day she started work. I remember that day very well. It was a cold and windy day in late January, a Monday. Mr. Johnson, the dock supervisor, and Cindy walked over to the truck I was loading. I put the box down and faced them.

"Casey this is Cindy." Cindy appeared more than a little nervous, almost scared. "This is her first day. Show her the ropes." Before I could answer Mr. Johnson turned to Cindy and continued. "Casey is a good worker. Most of the time he'll run the other guys into the ground. However, under no circumstance mention two words. Harley-Davidson. If you do he just stops whatever he's doing." Without a further word Mr. Johnson turned and walked to his office.

"So Casey," Cindy said with a grin, "I cannot mention a certain American motorcycle company?"

"Oh, you can mention a certain American motorcycle company," I stated, "however, you'll then have to listen to me talk about the merits and products of that certain American motorcycle company. And listen for hours. And hours." Cindy smiled and seemed to relax.

I have to give Cindy credit, she learned fast and she was a good worker. She was always on time and ready to go to work. She also never complained which was a far cry from some of our co-workers.

There is something else I have to give Cindy credit for. For an older woman she looked better than many of the girls I went to college with. Cindy was lean, long legged and blonde, which in my book is a pretty good combination at any age.

Cindy and I worked well together. Though we joked and laughed a lot we always carried more than our fair share of the load. Whenever the work permitted we took our breaks and meals together. We talked about everything under the sun-politics, sports, places we visited, my planned bike ride, everything but that certain American motorcycle company. Needless to say Cindy and I quickly became good friends.

About the second week that she was working Cindy called me at home. "I hope you don't mind," she began. "No. Not at all," I assured her. As I was only working a full day Monday and Thursday afternoon Cindy wanted to give me a heads up on what to expect when I returned to work the following afternoon.

"Tomorrow is going to be rough," she stated. "Mr. Johnson fired Tommy and that red haired guy."

"No surprise there. Both were worthless." I remarked.

"Well, I just wanted to let you know."

I thanked her. "Anytime you want to talk please call."

Cindy wanted to talk. We spent more than an hour on the phone that night. It was the first of many telephone conversations we had over the coming months.

Around the middle of March the temperature began to rise, the snow melted and a good rain washed the salt off of roads. In my mind it was nature's way of proclaiming the start of the riding season. I went into the garage and reinstalled the battery in the super glide.

The next morning I rode my bike to college and then to work. As I pulled into the parking lot I could see Cindy standing on the dock watching me. She was smiling.

When I joined her she greeted me. "I'm happy that you're finally able to ride your motorcycle." She said.

"So am I. It has been a long and cold winter. But, I think it's over." I remarked with relief.

"After work I'd like to see your bike so don't go riding off into the blue." She commanded with a twinkle in her eyes.

"Yes mam!" I answered with a salute.

Cindy was true to her word. She not only listened to my fifty cent tour of the FXD, she even pretended to be interested! When I finished Cindy gave the bike a thorough looking over. "It's a very pretty motorcycle." She commented.

"I think so too." I stated, then quickly added. "It's a sweet bike and a sweet runner."

Cindy laughed. "I never heard a motorcycle described as sweet before."

"Well, it is." I answered with certainty in my voice.

The slender blonde smiled. "I hope you have a lot of sweet rides on your sweet running motorcycle."

We both laughed.

"Would you like to go for a ride?" I asked.

Cindy thought for a moment then declined. "But thank you for the invitation."

"Anytime you want to go for a ride just let me know."

"I just may surprise you." Cindy said with a hint of promise in her voice.

By the beginning of April I figured that I had saved more than enough money for my bike vacation. Cindy was the only reason I continued to work. However, as the weather got warmer greater became the urge to quit. Nevertheless I stayed on the loading dock until the day before my last final exam.

When I punched out for the last time Cindy handed me a small gift wrapped box.

"What's this?" I asked.

"It's something I thought you might need on your bike ride." Cindy answered.

I opened it up. Inside was a pass to the national parks and a brochure with all the parks listed. I was pleasantly surprised. "Thank you. Thank you very much. That was a thoughtful gift."

Cindy smiled. "I've never been to a national park, so you'll have to tell me about them when you return."

"I most certainly will."

"I'm glad you like it." Cindy stated. "I didn't know what to get you. I kept thinking you'd be gone before I got you something. The idea for the pass only came to me last week when we were talking about Arizona and the Grand Canyon."

"Well I'm glad you thought of it. It's a very nice gift and I'll use it. I promise."

"I didn't think you'd work this long, but I'm glad you did."

"Neither did I." I confessed. "I only stayed because I was hoping to take you for a ride. But I guess that is not to be."

Cindy feigned being hurt. "You haven't asked me but that one time."

"Well that one time you said you might just surprise me."

A smile came over Cindy's face. "When and where do you want to go on this ride?" She asked.

"Tomorrow night. Gary and I are celebrating the end of school. It's also a farewell party-I leave Monday morning. Anyway, we're riding to a bar in Jersey. It's supposed to have a good band." Then I quickly added, "And lots of women too." Instantly I felt like an idiot.

Cindy was silent for a moment. When she spoke there was sadness in her voice.

"Friday would have been my 15th wedding anniversary."

Her words seemed to just hang in the air. It took a long time for them to vanish.

"I'm sorry," I said softly then added: "If you still want to go we'll have a good time." I assured her.

Cindy tried but couldn't stifle a laugh.

"What's so funny?" I asked.

"I appreciate the fact that you're trying to cheer me up. I really do. And I really want to go for a ride, however, taking me to a bar where there are lots of women doesn't do it for me. Besides, I'm sure you'd rather dance with a girl your age than with an old lady like me."

Without hesitation I asked her a simple question. "Where would I have to take you to cheer you up?"

Cindy looked at me long and hard.

"To a bar in Jersey that's supposed to have a good band. But, in your eyes the only woman in that bar is me."

I nodded my head in the affirmative. "Agreed."

"One other thing," Cindy continued, "we're going as friends. Nothing more."

Again I nodded my head in the affirmative. "Friends."

Gary wasn't surprised when I told him I was taking Cindy with me. "Hell, she's all you ever talk about," was his only comment. Not to be odd man out Gary showed up at my house Friday night packing Keri.

It was a fun night. Gary saw to that. First, he got us lost. Then his sportster ran out of gas. However, luck was with us. Not more than fifty feet in front of Gary's dead 1200 was a gas station. And more luck was with us when the attendant told us how to get to the elusive bar. Pointing to a nondescript building practically directly across the street he asked, "You see that building?" Before anyone could answer he continued. "That's it."

The band, as advertised, was very good. Their repertoire was a combination of sixties and seventies music. Cindy had said that she came to dance and she certainly wasted no time in doing so. As soon as we found a table she took my hand and led us onto the dance floor.

Cindy would have stayed until the band called it a night and the bar closed. However, she changed her mind when we stepped outside to get a breath of fresh air. "It's cold." She stated to which I quickly added, "And it's only going to get colder." Cindy put two and two together. We went back inside the bar and told Gary and Keri our decision. They chose to stay. Cindy and I put on our jackets and grabbed our helmets.

It quickly became evident that our denim jackets were no match for the night air. It was a miserable ride. After what seemed an eternity in a very cold hell I parked the super glide in front of Cindy's apartment complex. Neither of us moved; we were frozen in place. Finally and ever so slowly we got off the bike. The walk to her apartment was almost painful.

At the door Cindy fumbled with the key. "Shit." She said in frustration. It brought a smile to my lips. It was the first time I ever heard Cindy swear. She finally inserted the key correctly and opened the door. Then Cindy turned to me.

"I'll make us some coffee and then you're going home." There was no mistaking her voice. It was all seriousness. We went inside her apartment. After some small talk and two cups of coffee I left.

The half hour ride home was only slightly less miserable then had been the hour plus ride to Cindy's place. However, it was still a miserable ride. When I finally got to my apartment all I wanted to do was take a hot shower and get under the covers. As I crawled into bed I noticed that the telephone answering machine was blinking. "See you in the morning." I commented. Within minutes I was fast asleep.

I would have slept longer but for a nagging in the back of my brain. It kept at me until it woke me. For a minute or two I relaxed, getting my thoughts together. Then it hit me, the reason for the nagging. "Damn!" I shouted as I jumped out of bed. The super glide had a ten o'clock service appointment. It was now five after nine and the dealership was a good 30 miles distant.

I was dressed and on my bike in record time. The traffic lights must have known that I was in a hurry; all were green. And the cops must have known that I was in a hurry; all were at their favorite donut shops. Only my bike's 96 inch twin cam engine conspired against me. It made me stop for gas. Still I made it to the shop on time.

No sooner had I shut down my bike then Joe took it by the handlebars and rolled it into the bay. I didn't stick around long, I was hungry. I walked down the street to a corner diner that served a great breakfast. I spent nearly an hour there killing time. Finally, after my third cup of coffee and that many trips to the men's room I paid my tab and left. The next hour was spent casually thumbing through magazines in the public library. When the clock struck twelve I returned to the Harley shop.

Otto had just finished adding up the bill when I walked through the door. He signaled me to the counter. Handing me the bill he explained every charge. Like all my previous services there the bill was less than expected. However, Joe the mechanic did not cut any corners. The proof came ten minutes later as I blasted down the interstate. The Harley was an even sweeter ride than it had been before.

I might have ridden all day, however, rain clouds were starting to move in from the west. I headed for home. It was a wise decision. No sooner had I parked the super glide inside the garage then the heavens opened up. The rain came down in buckets. For the time being I was stuck in the garage. I made the best of a less than ideal situation; I got the cleaning supplies from the locker and went to work on my bike.

Time passes quickly when you're doing something you enjoy. Though I am not a clean freak like Gary, I still derive satisfaction from cleaning my bike. And that Harley certainly needed a good cleaning.

It was nearly two thirty when I put the cleaning supplies back in the closet. Before leaving the garage I did a final walk around of the bike. It looked good-almost pristine. I closed the garage door and ran to my apartment. It was still raining.

The phone was ringing when I opened the door. It was Gary.

"Been calling you all morning. Didn't you get my message? How did it go last night with you and Cindy?" He asked.

"Things went as expected. Cindy and I are just friends." I stated.

Gary laughed, then switched subjects. He and Keri were going to the movies that evening and wanted to know if Cindy and I wanted to join them.

"Thanks, but no thanks," I replied. Gary did not press the matter. We hung up with plans to get together for a ride tomorrow. "If the rain ever stops."

I went into the bathroom to wash the grease and wax from my hands. When I finished I grabbed the keys to the Ranger and tossed on my Yankees hat. As I walked past the phone I noticed that the recorder was flashing. I pressed the erase button and instantly realized that I had erased not only Gary's message but the message that had been blinking when I came home earlier that morning. "Oh well," I muttered as I went out the door. Ten minutes later I was parking the Ford in the lot of my favorite Italian restaurant.

The rain stopped late that night. The following morning Gary and I got together for a last ride.

"You're a lucky guy," Gary stated as we filled our bikes. "Taking the summer off to ride your new Harley cross country."

"Not lucky," I corrected my friend. "Fortunate and smart." I paused to pay the attendant. When the teenager handed me my change I continued. "Fortunate that I didn't get killed in Iraq last year. Smart enough to take advantage of what I earned." Later that afternoon I packed my bike in anticipation of an early morning departure.

Monday dawned sunny and warm. I took it as a harbinger of what I could expect on my cross country ride. I ate breakfast with my parents then got on the road. It was a few minutes after seven when the super glide took the on ramp to the interstate.

My summer odyssey was a dream come true. Thanks to Cindy I had a reason to stop at every national park, battlefield and monument I happened upon. The first day I visited two; Antietam and Harpers Ferry. That night I wrote a brief letter to Cindy. Included in the letter were half a dozen post cards and the brochures from the two sites. A similar letter was sent to my parents.

Over the course of the next seven weeks my travels took me through more than twenty states and to scores of our national treasures. Each night I would write Cindy about that days travels. I tried calling her a couple of times; however she never answered the phone. It just rang and rang. I even thought of trying to reach her at work but thought better of it. Mr. Johnson did not like people taking personal phone calls on company time.

Knowing how much Cindy wanted to see the Grand Canyon I went out of my way to visit it. It was well worth the effort. The ride from Phoenix to the north rim was spectacular as was the abyss. The next morning I mailed Cindy a package that included three books about the canyon that I thought she would enjoy reading.

In southern California I met up with a friend from the army. Tom and I served in the same tank in the states and in Iraq. He was the gunner and I was the loader. After we returned to Fort Riley Tom was drafted to be a recruiter. He left for recruiter's school a few days after I got out of the army. At first Tom wasn't thrilled about being a recruiter; however, he came to like the job. In fact he had taken to it like a duck to water. Tom was now wearing the rocker of a staff sergeant and he was the station commander of a three man station. "It's great here," he explained as we sat at his desk. "The weather is always nice. Women are plentiful, beautiful and friendly. What more could a guy want?"

I stayed at Tom's Garden Grove apartment for three days. The following afternoon I brought the bike to the local Harley dealer for a service. While the bike was being worked on I went for a walk. After nearly four thousand miles in the saddle it felt great to stretch my legs. Passing a convenience store I went inside to buy some post cards. After paying for them I stepped outside and spotted a pay phone booth. In the spur of the moment I decided to call Cindy. I dialed her number and deposited the correct amount of change. A recording came on and announced that the number had been disconnected. I immediately called her place of work. Mr. Johnson answered. As soon as I identified myself he bluntly told me that Cindy had quit. "Her last day was the same as yours." I was stunned.

From Garden Grove I headed north to Los Angeles. Every since hearing the Door's "LA Woman" I've always wanted to ride a Harley in the city of lights. I thought it would be cool. However, the traffic was horrible, the pollution palpable and the heat oppressive. It most definitely failed to live up to expectations. It was not a fun ride.

Finally free of the city I jumped on the interstate to make up for lost time. After an hour of freeway blasting I exited and headed west towards the ocean. I didn't make it far.

He was standing on the side of the road. Next to him was his motorcycle. I stopped a short distance past him. "You look like you could use some help," I called as I got off the super glide.

As I approached him he mumbled something, but I didn't catch it. Then he gestured to his bike. Under it was a black pool, the oil that should have been in the motor. I let out a whistle. "We got a problem here."

It quickly became apparent that neither bike or rider should have been on the road. Fred, I think that was his name, was even in worse shape then his panhead. He was a wreck from head to toe. Fred had not been wearing a helmet; his hair looked like he had moistened his finger then stuck it in an electrical outlet. The day was hotter than hell yet he was riding sans a shirt. Plastered to his sun burnt chest were smashed bugs and road grime. His torn and oil splattered pants were worn way too low. However, the item that tied everything together was his stomach. It hung over the front of his pants like a giant blob. And like his chest, Fred's massive stomach, was sun burnt and plastered with smashed bugs and road grime. I doubt a less attractive stomach was ever seen in public.

Fred was also high. He told me so after we pushed his bike into the parking lot of a strip mall. No sooner had I put the kick stand down then Fred took a seat on the curb. Immediately his arms fell to the ground and head hung limp on his chest. I thought he had fallen asleep. He hadn't. "Too much nose candy." He slurred.

Unable to refrain myself I asked the obvious. "How were you able to ride?"

"It was easy," Fred responded without hesitation. His raised his arms and grabbed onto imaginary handlebars. Then he turned the bars from side to side. "Easy," he said as his hands once again fell to the ground. At no time did his head come off his chest. I could not stifle a laugh.

I didn't laugh long. Within a millisecond a cop car pulled into the parking lot. The door opened and out stepped Barney Fife's twin. However, unlike the bumpkin who he happened to look like, this Barney Fife was all business.

The cop asked me a couple of questions, then satisfied with my answers, pointed to my bike. "Get on it and get out of here." He commanded. I took his advise. As I was strapping on my helmet the cop was busy handcuffing Fred.

I made it to Watsonville the following morning. Watsonville is a farming town about ninety miles south of San Francisco. It is also home to my favorite aunt, aunt Nellie. How my Pennsylvania born and raised aunt came to live in California is a funny story. A couple of years ago she entered a contest and won. First prize was a week in San Francisco. After seeing the sights of the city by the bay aunt Nellie set out to drive to Los Angeles. She only made it to Watsonville. There she had a fender bender; fortunately neither she nor the other driver was hurt. The other driver just happened to be the head nurse at the local hospital. Aunt Nellie is a nurse. The rest is history.

It was while at aunt Nellie's that I realized I was fast running out of money. Though I had been pretty frugal I nevertheless was down to my reserves. I figured that I had enough money left for six, maybe seven days on the road. Riding to Seattle and Mount Rainier would have to wait for another time.

Four days after knocking on aunt Nellie's door I left. However, not before I fulfilled another one of my 'must do' experiences. On an incredibly beautiful day I rode across the Golden Gate Bridge. It was a bit cool, but, infinitely more enjoyable than my ride through LA had been.

I made excellent time riding home. From early morning to after sunset I rode. My only stops were for gas and meals. Except for a brief rain storm in Iowa the weather cooperated.

During those near endless hours on the interstate my mind wandered. One minute I was naming the national parks I had visited, the next minute I would be figuring out my gas mileage. And of course I often wondered about Cindy. Where she had gone to, would she try to contact me? Thoughts of her were especially strong when paying for gas. Inevitably there would be post cards in the gas station. It felt odd not buying duplicates.

It took me a little better than four days to cross America. It was three thirty in the morning when I put the FXD's kick stand down in my garage. I was frazzled.

I spent the next couple of days relaxing. And reading my mail. Buried in the pile of credit card applications, motorcycle magazines and junk mail was a letter from Cindy. I tore it open.

"Casey I want to thank you for last Friday night. It was a lot of fun and it definitely cheered me up. You made me feel that I was the only woman in the bar. I'm pretty sure that you were more than a little miffed by the way I gave you the bums rush in my apartment. Believe me I very much wanted you to stay. However, I think we both know it would be wrong. That pesky age thing again. I wanted to tell you that, but didn't know how. That's why I called your apartment after you left. I kept waiting for you to call but you never did. I guess you were either too tired or too angry. I know you will meet a beautiful YOUNG lady who you will love and who will love you. Thanks from the bottom of my heart for making an old lady feel special. Love, Cindy. PS. As you probably know by now I too quit my job. I've moved back to Vermont to live with my sister."

Cindy was right. The first day of college I met a beautiful YOUNG lady. She was standing behind me in the line at the student cafeteria. I turned, smiled and said hello. She smiled and said hello. Then we both laughed. At that instant we both knew that we had found our soul mate. Funny thing, her name is Cindy.

Mr. Butlers' 36 EL

Two summers ago Tommy and I bought the Breeze. We had always wanted to own a biker bar and the Breeze was definitely a biker bar. It had been one from its inception. William Butler was a successful banker who moved here from back east. Butler loved three things; making money, riding his Harley and drinking the liquid gold that made Milwaukee famous. The story goes that Butler would set out on his Harley every Saturday morning for a ride in the mountains. However, before noon he would have to turn around and head back to town. The reason? There wasn't a bar in the area where he was riding that served a decent beer. After the second or third time that he had to cut short his bike riding day Butler decided to do something about it. He knew what had to be done to remedy "this unbearable situation." Those were his words as quoted by the Sun newspaper. The answer to this problem would satisfy all three of his loves. He would make money, he would ride his Harley and he would drink the golden hops. Half an hours drive outside of town was a piece of land the bank had foreclosed on. A piece of land Butler was going to build a bar on.

Three months later the Breeze was pouring beer to thirsty bikers and factory workers. It was rumored that Butler was his own best customer. He was what barkeeps would call a 'regular regular.' He started spending more time at the bar and less time at the bank. It was also well known that his wife was highly annoyed at his excursions. She wanted him off his motorcycle and home. However, that did not stop him. Butler would ride to the Breeze most every night after the bank closed. The only effect his wife's harping had on him was to make him drink his beer that much faster. If Mrs. Butler could not stop her husbands' bike riding and beer drinking the grim reaper could. The end came less than six months after the Breeze opened its' door. His obituary states that he died when his motorcycle failed to negotiate a curve and crashed into a tree. The accident occurred a few minutes after sunset on a cool spring evening in 1938. William Butler lost his life a little more than a mile from the bar he brought to life.

Butler's son, William Jr., was not a biker. He was a banker, and a more successful one than his father. The depression was ending and the Second World War was looming large. People were working and the banking business was booming. A nearby army base put a lot of money into the local economy, much of which ended up in Butlers' First Republic Bank. Junior, twenty-two and just out of college when his dad died, did not have the time or the inclination to oversee a bar. On Friday, December 5, 1941 he signed the deed to the Breeze over to Frank Walton. Walton, like the late Butler, was a Harley rider.

Walton was also an avid photographer. He evidently was a pretty good one too. A year or so before he bought the Breeze the senior Butler and Walton came to an agreement. It was an enticement to get customers in and keep them coming back. Walton would set up his camera in the Breezes' parking lot. When a biker rolled in he would offer them a free beer for their consent for immortality. Very few bikers can refuse a free beer, so most if not all who stopped had their picture taken. Walton would then frame and hang the picture inside the bar. The two partners believed the biker would be grateful for the free beer and more importantly would want to return with his friends to show off his picture and probably buy a beer or two.

The pictures and frames were of very good quality. Both Butler and Walton knew you had to spend money in order to make money. Included in the frame was a strip of paper that answered three questions. Who was pictured, the model of motorcycle and the date the photograph was taken. No more, no less.

The first pictures were hung behind the bar. "The place of honor," Walton called it. From there the picture parade went down the hallway to the pool room. Pictures were hung from knee high to shoulder height. They were hung on the doors to the cleaning closet, both bathrooms and the office. When the pool room was filled the other side of the hallway was covered. Then it was back to the barroom which today is about half filled. No one has ever counted the pictures but someone guessed that there were close to a thousand.

When Walton sold the Breeze in 1968 he had written into the contract that the pictures were not to be disturbed or moved. The new owner, Virgil Rogers, was more than happy to comply. The 'Breeze collection' as it was called, had been featured in two biker magazines. People from all over the country stopped in to check out the collection of bike pictures. Many bought a beer or two. And bikers still more came to have their pictures taken.

In the late sixties and early seventies guys started showing up at the Breeze on Jap bikes. Virgil, just back from Vietnam and very much into Harley's, wouldn't even offer to take their picture. One guy, Virgil related to me, got into a beef with him over his refusal to shoot his Honda. The guy finally got the point after Virgil punched him out. Among the hundreds of pictures there is not one foreign motorcycle. Most, but not all, are Harley-Davidsons. The others are Indians and other less known American made bikes. One could learn a lot about the Motor Company and the biker lifestyle by checking out the black and white photographs that adorned the walls of the Breeze.

Virgil and I became friends shortly after I returned from the first Gulf War. I was nursing a beer one muggy Friday afternoon. Virgil was tending bar. We started talking, nothing in particular. An hour later we're laughing like old high school buddies. It wasn't the fact that we both rode Harley's, what opened the floodgate of good will was the fact that we both served in the first infantry division. Virgil had been a grunt and I had been a tanker in the 'Big Red One'. From then on anytime I entered the Breeze Virgil and I would greet each other with 'if you're going to be one, be a big red one!' The other patrons though it was amusing.

I never knew my real dad. He had walked out on the family when I was six months old. A year later my mother remarried. Her new husband was a real jerk. He didn't care for me and the feeling was mutual. Two days after I graduated from high school they moved to Alaska. I wasn't there to wave goodbye to them, the day before I had left for the army. I haven't heard from either my father or mother in years and I don't expect a letter from them anytime soon.

Over the years Virgil became almost a surrogate father to me. We rode together more than a couple of times, he on his dresser and me on my sportster. And as bonding as that may be, Virgil was more than just another riding partner. He was there for me when it counted. He was there when my GI Bill checks suddenly stopped and I was penniless. He opened up his cash register and wrote me a check for five hundred dollars. "Pay me back when you can," was all he said. The night I received my degree in elementary education he was in the audience cheering for me. When I applied for a teaching position at the local elementary school he put in a good word with the principal. The principal was another Vietnam veteran Virgil grew up with. And two years ago when Virgil confessed that he was thinking of selling the Breeze and retiring to Hawaii I was the first one he told.

"Go for it." I said with enthusiasm.

The grizzled biker/barkeep nodded. "Only thing keeping me here is here," he said gesturing to the four walls.

Without hesitation I blurted out, "I'll buy the Breeze." Then I quickly added, "Tommy and I will buy the Breeze."

"What about your job as a teacher?" Virgil asked.

"Teaching is a day job, the Breeze is a night job. Tommy and I will work it out."

That seemed to satisfy my good friend. He smiled. "If you're going to be one," he started and we both finished. "Be a big red one."

Tommy and I met in college. He had parked his super glide next to my sportster and we started talking. He had just gotten out of the air force. "Four years in Minot, North Dakota," he joked, "was far worse than any war in Iraq." Tommy graduated with a degree in history and intentions of teaching. However, he didn't have a patron saint like Virgil. Within a year he had given up getting a teaching job and instead started a house painting business. Things went well for the first couple of years, then Tommy slipped off a ladder and hurt his back. Every since that day he talked about getting out of the business. More than one night we sat at the Breezes' bar and joked about owning the place. Tommy liked the beer and I liked the women who frequented the Breeze.

Virgil calls from Hawaii every few weeks and about that often we get a post card or letter from him. He's doing well, riding and surfing. "It was tough," he confessed in one of his first letters, "but I don't regret my decision to sell the Breeze." That afternoon I wrote back. "It was tough for us too. And like you, we do not regret our decision to buy the Breeze."

In the two years we've owned the breeze I've seen some funny things happen inside its brick walls. Funny and stupid things. Like the day two guys on brand new electra glides couldn't start their bikes. The two guys experienced the same problem-they couldn't insert the key into the ignition to unlock their bikes. Try as they might it was a no go for both of them. After five or ten minutes of cursing they came back inside and took the seats they had just vacated at the bar. "What's up?" I asked. They told me their problem and the fact that they had just called the Harley dealer. "They're going to send a mechanic out when one returns from lunch." The heavier of the two riders stated. I nodded and went about my business. Then I caught a glimpse of their bikes. The two were identical, jet black. "Give me your keys," I stated, "and call the dealer and tell him to save his gas." I took the keys and walked to the bikes. The first key did not fit the ignition slot, however the second key fit it perfectly. Then I went to the next bike and inserted the key into the ignition slot. It too fit perfectly. A moment later both bikes were idling. When the two guys heard their engines they joined me. Both were incredulous. "How did you do it?" They asked. "You were trying to start each other's bike." I explained with a laugh.

I've also seen some sad things happen at the Breeze. Like the night a limo pulled up at the door. Out jumps the chauffer who quickly opens the back door. A very well dressed man steps out of the car. Not the typical Breeze customer. When he enters I call to him. "Cold day today." He smiles at my attempt at humor. The temperature was well into the nineties. He sits at the bar and orders a beer. "Coming right up." The guy drinks almost as if he was being forced to. I start to say something, then think better of it. I go back to watching the ball game on the television. Stealing a glance at the guy it's clear that he wants to be left alone. Then I notice he's crying. First a tear or two then a flood cascades down his cheeks. I slide a box of tissues his way. He takes one, looks up at me.

"Pretty crappy beer," I say in jest as the man dries his tears.

"Pretty crappy beer," he repeats. He's smiling.

"I know. That's why I don't drink it." I pause for a moment then ask. "Anything you want to talk about?"

He nods his head. "My father," he starts off in a low, monotone voice, "used to work in a factory in town. Every payday he and his buddies would drive here and drink beer. He worked in that factory forty years. And probably every Friday night for forty years he came here. And drank beer with his buddies." The man paused, took a sip of his beer. "I hate beer." He remarked.

"Why did you order it?" I inquired.

The man took a deep breath. When he continued it was evident he was happier then he was just a minute ago.

"My dad told me to have a beer tonight at the Breeze."

I nodded. "Sounds like a good dad."

"He died yesterday. Lung cancer."

I didn't know what to say, so I kept quiet. After what seemed an eternity the customer broke the silence.

"A few days before dad died he touched my hand. He was in the hospital; he knew he didn't have much time. He wanted to say something so I leaned my ear next to his mouth. He said he wishes he had been a better father. That he should have done more things with me. Played catch, talked with me, things like that. Then he says there is one thing he'd like me to do. Have a beer in the Breeze and toast him." The man was crying again, this time softly. But he was also smiling. Then he started laughing. When he stopped laughing he hoisted his glass of Miller above his head. "Here's to you dad!" He took a long pull; slammed the empty glass onto the bar. "Damn, I feel better!" He exclaimed with enthusiasm. He seemed relieved, relieved that he and his father had at long last bonded. Then he wiped his face, threw a twenty on the bar. Moments later I watched as he walked out the door. He never looked back.

Without a doubt the strangest thing ever to happen to me happened last night. And it happened here at the Breeze. Every night at 7:53 sharp a biker would ride in from town and park his scooter by the door. You could set your watch by this guy. Rain or shine he was there and it was always 7:53 on the nose. Once inside he'd take a look around. Satisfied he would then sit at the bar and put down a buck. It was assumed that he wanted a beer for he never spoke.

He would down his one beer, give a quick glance around the bar then leave. Like his arrival it was always at the same time; 8:08. So far there's nothing too strange about the guy. I figured he was just another thirsty biker of few words who happened to be very punctual. All the employees and many of the customers knew the guys' habit. However, no one knew him. No one had ever gotten a simple hello out of him. Everyone simply called him 'Mr. 7:53' or 'Mr. Strange.'

About a week ago Mike, my panhead-riding friend from way back, happened to catch Mr. 7:53's bike parked by the door. A minute later Mike buttonholed me. He could hardly contain himself. "Man," he stated breathlessly, "there's a '36 EL out there that is absolutely cherry. And I'll be damned if it isn't just as it was the day it rolled out of Milwaukee." My excited friend dragged me from behind the bar and out the door. I confess; I'm no Harley expert. Mike is though, and if he says the bike in front of us was not just a knucklehead, but a first year knucklehead, then it's a first year knucklehead.

While I casually walked around the bike Mike gave me the history of the 61 inch V-twin. "Thanks for the ten cent tour," I stated as I reached for the door. "There are people inside who need my help escaping from reality," I explained with a grin. I opened the door and nearly collided with Mr. 7:53. "Excuse me," I said. Mr. 7:53 looked at me like I wasn't there. Suddenly, and I'll swear this on a Bible, I was enveloped in a cloud of ice-cold air. The hair on the back of my neck stood straight up. Mike started to say something to the man but his words were drowned out by the rumble of the knucklehead coming to life.

A couple of nights later Tommy and I were shooting the bull when Mr. 7:53 came up. "He came in tonight. Right on time. Had his beer, checked the place out, then left. 8:08 on the nose." Tommy related to me. I started to laugh harder and harder. Tommy looked at me wondering what was so funny. When I finally regained my composure I told my partner that I had an idea. "At 7:52 we should set the clocks to 8:08. When our friend walks in he won't know whether he's coming or going." Tommy laughed, but we didn't change the bars' one clock.

I'm not a great bartender. However, in a beer and shot joint like the Breeze I can hold my own. Not every customer who walks through the door knows what kind of bar we are. The guy who took a seat at the end of the bar last night certainly didn't know. He ordered some flaming something or another. "Sorry pal," I explained to the guy, "if it doesn't come out of a keg or a whiskey bottle you're out of luck." He shrugged his shoulders then ordered a beer. I happened to glance at the clock; it was 7:53. The door opened and in walked our most regular of regular customers. True to form he paused a moment while he looked around the bar. Then satisfied he took the seat next to the guy who had ordered the exotic drink. A smile crept over my face as I started pouring a second beer.

After I placed the beer in front of Mr. 7:53 I went to the other end of the bar. It was a slow night so I took the opportunity to study the knucklehead riding biker. He was of average height and lean of build. His hair was short and graying at the temples. Under his old style leather-riding jacket he wore a tie. I would guess he was in his late forties or early fifties. And as long as I'm guessing I would say he was a successful businessman or perhaps a banker. He had to be, I reasoned, who else could afford a pristine '36 EL?

Mr. Exotic turned to and said something to Mr. 7:53. Though I couldn't hear his exact words it sounded like, 'how's it going?' However, Mr. 7:53 more than just ignored the man, he acted as if the man did not exist. Taking the not very subtle hint Mr. Exotic went back to his beer. When he polished it off he signaled for another. I refilled his glass. "On the house," I rolled my eyes and tilted my head in the direction of Mr. 7:53. The new customer smiled. At 8:08 when Mr. Strange got up to leave his beer drinking neighbor didn't bat an eye.

I picked up the dollar bill Mr. 7:53 left by his empty glass. "Don't mind that guy," I stated to Mr. Exotic. "He's pretty strange."

"He's a strange one all right." The guy said with a snicker. He took a sip of his beer then blurted out something that caught my interest.

"I just wanted to point out that it was a good picture of him."

"What picture?" I asked.

Mr. Exotic pointed. I turned.

"Above the cash register." Mr. Exotic stated.

There was but one picture hanging above the cash register and I picked it up.

I glanced at it then handed the picture to the customer. "This guy?" I asked.

The customer studied the picture, but only for a moment. When he spoke he did so with certainty in his voice. "I was a street cop for 30 years. I can recognize a face. That guy," he gestured to the empty seat next to him, "is the guy in this picture."

I took back the picture. For the first time ever I looked closely at it. I had glanced at it countless times while ringing the cash register, but I never studied it. I did now though. Suddenly my hands began to tremble. "I'll be," I muttered in disbelief. "It is. It really is him." I held the first picture ever taken of a biker at the Breeze. It was also the only picture with more than three pieces of information on it. Included with the name of the rider, the motorcycle model and the date the picture was taken the following was typed: "He lived life to the fullest and died with a glass of beer in him and his Harley under him. Rest in peace. April 17, 1938." The picture was of William Butler.

Thanks For The Bikes

Cindy was teaching her second graders math when the classroom phone rang. Walking to the phone she signaled to Mrs. Brown to continue the lesson. The diminutive aide nodded then called out the next problem.

"Mrs. Wilson speaking," Cindy spoke into the phone.

The schools principal was on the other end. He wasted no time. "Your husband has been taken to the hospital. You need to go there now. Mrs. Tomack will take over your class."

Hanging up the phone Cindy went quickly to her desk. As she picked up her purse Mrs. Tomack entered the classroom.

Before disappearing out the door Cindy turned to her children. All 23 sets of young eyes were on her. "I have to go. Listen to Mrs. Tomack and Mrs. Brown."

Cindy hurried to the hospital; however, she was too late. "I'm very sorry Mrs. Wilson," the distinguished looking doctor told her, "but your husband died."

Cindy came back to work on a Friday. "I wanted to start off slow," she explained to Mrs. Brown. The aide smiled. "Sounds like a good idea. The little people will be happy to have you back. They missed you."

"I missed them too," Cindy confessed, holding back a tear.

After school Cindy and Debbie walked to the corner deli together. 'The Country Corner' was the unofficial gathering place and news headquarters for the tight knit community of Webster. If it happened anywhere in town you'd hear about it in the 'Corner.'

The two sister and had a long tradition. Every Friday they would go to the 'Corner' and over coffee and cake talk. It was very important to them. They called it their sister time.

The past year had been a traumatic one. The sisters had always been close, now they were even closer. Cindy had been there for Debbie when her husband left her. "One day Roger came home from work and started packing his belongings." Debbie had confined in Cindy. "I asked what he was doing. Roger merely looked at me and said he didn't love me anymore and that he was leaving. He had fallen in love with that 22 year old whore Maria, the secretary in his office." The shock of it had nearly driven Debbie into a depression.

Now Debbie was there for Cindy. Over apple pie covered with whipped cream the younger sister confessed she was emotionally spent. "I'm going through the motions," she said. "I'm very lucky Mrs. Brown is there. She carried me today." Debbie sat silently, listening to her sister as she related the events of her day that had caused her so much anguish.

When she finished Debbie touched her sisters' hands. "Yes, you are very lucky to have such a good aide. Mrs. Brown is a God send. And she's very lucky too. Lucky that she is your aide. You're a good teacher, a great teacher. Everyone knows it. Today was your first day back in three weeks. Tomorrow, Monday will be better. And the day after that you'll be better still. Trust me."

Debbie was right. The following Monday Cindy was the energetic, funny and incredibly patient teacher she had been from the day she started work at Webster elementary school 12 years ago. As she led her class to the lunch room Matthew got her attention. "You didn't have to write my name on the board once," he proudly proclaimed. "And you're not going to anymore. I don't want to upset you." Coming from the class trouble maker Cindy was nearly speechless. "Thank you," was all she could say.

The first seeds were planted innocently enough one Saturday night as the two sisters talked on the telephone.

"Thelma and Louise, is on tonight," Debbie mentioned.

Cindy commented that she liked the movie. Then added, "Except for the end. And the fact that they shot a man."

Debbie laughed. "I thought the best part of the movie was when they shot the guy." The two sisters laughed.

"I've wanted to see the Grand Canyon for as long as I can remember," Cindy related. "One of these years Mike and I were going to make it. That is unless he was going to be deployed to Iraq again."

"Hey, here's an idea. Why don't we go next summer? We're teachers remember, we get the summer off."

Cindy was silent. Finally Debbie asked, "You still there sis?'

"Yes. Still here," answered Cindy. "Let's give it some thought."

The following Friday as they took their usual seats in the 'Corner' Cindy stated that she had looked into it.

"Looked into what?" inquired her sister.

Before answering Cindy took from her purse an article cut from a travel magazine. "The Grand Canyon. I went on the internet and read about it. And today I found this in the teachers lounge." Cindy handed Debbie the article. When Debbie finished reading it she placed it on the table.

"I'm convinced. Do you want me to make the reservations? Airplane, hotel, rental car."

"Not so fast," Cindy said. "I was thinking about the movie Thelma and Louise."

"Oh no," Debbie groaned.

"Oh no, what?" Cindy asked.

Debbie looked her sister straight in the face. "I love you kid. And there's only one thing I won't do for you. And that one thing is drive off the Grand Canyon."

Cindy laughed out loud. "You thought I thought," she said as she tried to regain her composure. "That I wanted us to." She finally gave up trying to explain herself and just laughed. When she finally stopped laughing her face was streaked with tears. Her sister handed her a paper napkin.

"Thank you. Sorry, if you thought I wanted us to go out like Thelma and Louise."

Debbie accepted her apology. "You had me worried," she confessed.

"What I wanted to say was, like the movie which shall remain nameless, I thought why not do a road trip. See some of this country of ours. I found a book in the library that has every national park in it. There are a lot I'd love to see."

Before they left the deli that day the two sisters had a plan. Each woman would pick out national parks and other points of interest they would like to see. Then the following Friday instead of going to the 'Corner' they would go to Debbie's house and using her computer plot a course to the sites they had selected. "We have all summer, let's use all of it," Cindy remarked as she hugged her sister good bye.

Debbie was beaming with excitement when she opened her door for Cindy. "I have nine national parks and two museums on my list," she proclaimed.

"That's great. I have seven national parks," Cindy stated as she followed her sister into the living room. They quickly took seats in front of the computer. A stack of maps and two cups of coffee and an apple pie were close by on a serving table.

"I already have my parks entered. Why don't you read off the names from your list?" Debbie instructed Cindy.

As she unfolded her list Cindy chuckled.

"What's so funny," asked her sister.

Cindy looked at her watch. "At this time every Friday for the past ten years we've met at the 'Corner.'" Cindy paused, cut a piece of pie. "Right now they're probably calling 911."

Cindy stayed for supper. They continued to pour over maps and enter data into the computer well into the night. Their planning was only interrupted by a phone call from Roger. It was a brief conversation. No sooner had Debbie said hello then she shouted into the phone, 'drop dead!' and slammed the phone down.

"The bastard," Debbie turned to her sister. She was visibly angered. "He called to ask for a reduction in alimony," Debbie said in disbelief.

"Are you sure you don't want to spend the night here?" Debbie asked Cindy. It was a few minutes past midnight.

Cindy shook her head. "Thanks. But I feel I have to be home." Debbie didn't quite understand, however, she wouldn't press her sister. "Drive carefully," was all she said.

Neither sister could sleep that night. Both were too wound up. They had put in a lot of work on their 'ultimate vacation.' The route they had settled on was in the words of Debbie 'incredible.' They would drive just under seven thousand miles through 23 states and visit a dozen national parks and two museums. They would leave the morning after the last day of school.

The following Friday Cindy and Debbie got together for sister time at the 'Corner.' When they entered the deli Nancy, the owner, spotted them. "I was wondering where you were last week. I almost called 911." The two sisters smiled.

One of the other regulars at the deli was an elder woman. Grandma M usually sat at the counter and drank her tea by herself. Today she was sitting at a table. It appeared as if she was expecting company. She was.

"My grandson is visiting. He'll be here any minute." The white haired woman announced to the other regulars gathered in the 'Corner.'

No sooner had Grandma M spoken then a rumble was heard from the parking lot. "That must be him," She said with excitement in her voice. Moments later the door opened and in walked a tall and very thin leather clad man. In one hand he held a motorcycle helmet. He looked about then strode across the room to his grandmother who warmly embraced him.

"You rode your motorcycle all the way from Atlanta just to see your grandmother? You're a good boy Bruce." Nancy stated as she placed his order in front of him. Slightly embarrassed Bruce meekly said 'yes.'

"What are you riding?" wondered John, another old time regular.

Bruce stopped from biting into his hamburger. "An electra glide ultra classic."

John pushed his Yankees hat to the back of his head, scratched his nose. "A what?" he asked.

"An electra glide ultra classic. It's a Harley-Davidson. Meant for riding long distances."

Bruce's answer seemed to satisfy John. The retired mechanic nodded as if he knew what he had been told. "A Harley-Davidson," he repeated then turned his attention back to the sandwich he had been eating.

Grandma M and her grandson were still talking when Cindy and Debbie got up to leave. "Good luck," Cindy called to the young man.

Outside the two sisters paused to look at Bruce's bright red motorcycle. "It's beautiful," Cindy commented.

"It even has a radio," Debbie announced with surprise in her voice.

"I bet it would be fun riding a motorcycle," Cindy remarked.

Debbie put her arm around her sister's shoulder. "Remember Thelma and Louise? Well there's a motorcycle movie that ends just as badly." When her younger sister showed no sign of recognition Debbie continued. "Peter Fonda. Dennis Hopper. Easy Rider. Remember?"

Cindy chuckled. "Oh yeah." She said slowly then quickly added, "But I bet it would still be fun to ride a motorcycle."

Debbie was adamant. "There is no way in the world you're going to get me on a motorcycle," she declared to her sister. They were having dinner in Cindy's house when the younger teacher broached the idea.

"I've talked with my neighbor down the street. Doug owns two Harley's. He said plenty of women ride. And that Harley makes motorcycles that are designed for women."

Debbie just shook her head. "I'm not listening to you."

"Now you're being just like some of my students," Cindy laughed. She left the table and went into the living room. When she returned she was holding a Harley-Davidson brochure. She opened it to a page she had tabbed.

"The sportster is one of the bikes Doug talked about. It's low to the ground and easy to handle."

Debbie studied the pictures of the motorcycles. "And how do you expect to learn to ride one of these?" she asked.

"At the motorcycle safety course I have us enrolled in," Cindy shot back.

Debbie looked at her sister with a blank expression. "What? How? When?" She finally stammered.

Cindy patted Debbie's hand. "Don't worry about a thing. I have everything covered," she assured her older sister.

Three weeks later the sisters were licensed motorcyclists. "All we need now are motorcycles," Debbie commented as Cindy started the car.

"Motorcycles here we come," Cindy answered with a smile that stretched from ear to ear.

Debbie was still shaking her head when they walked out of the Harley-Davidson dealership. "I can't believe it," she kept repeating. Cindy turned to her sister. "Believe it baby;" she said loudly, "you're now the proud owner of a brand new sportster 883."

"Oh, I can believe that," Debbie answered with a grin, "what I can't believe is that my little sister is the owner of a brand new sportster 883." The two women laughed uproarsly.

They didn't have many chances to ride before the bikes had to be parked for the winter. However, when spring came the two rode their motorcycles at every opportunity. Most weekends the two sisters went for a ride. They often put on more than a hundred miles at a stretch.

"We need to get comfortable with riding two hundred miles a day," Cindy stated as they gassed up their bikes.

Debbie nodded in agreement. "Next week they're putting on the highway pegs I ordered. That will let me stretch my legs. They're also putting on the sissy bar."

"That should help," Cindy commented as she tightened the cap on her gas tank.

Inserting the gas nozzle into the 883's gas tank Debbie nodded in agreement.

By the middle of June both Cindy and Debbie were comfortable with riding three hundred miles in a day. The Tuesday before they were to start their epic ride they rode their bikes to the dealership for a service. "Look at this," the service writer announced to a mechanic who just happened to walk by the front counter. "Both women are having their five k service done today. On new 883's." The mechanic seemed impressed. "That puts many a man to shame." He commented before continuing on his way. "He's right," added the service writer. "Lot's of guys don't put two thousand miles on their bikes all year."

"That's true," stated the mechanic who again happened to walk pass the front counter. "A guy was in last week on a two year old electra glide classic. He was dressed from head to toe in leather. Ear rings, chain wallet, the whole nine yards. The guy saunters in here like he was some bad assed biker."

"I remember him," the service writer interjected with a grin.

The mechanic continued with a story he obviously enjoyed telling. "Mr. Biker was here to schedule his first service. He had nine hundred fifty seven miles on his two year old bike."

The service writer shook his head in mock amazement. Then his demur turned series. Gesturing to Cindy and Debbie he loudly proclaimed, "We have here two bikers."

Neither sister knew what to say. Inside, each, felt that they had been accepted into a very special fraternity. Debbie later confessed that she felt honored. "I guess, no, I know we can do anything we want." Cindy had agreed wholeheartedly.

The news struck the small town hard. Many were in shock. The regulars at the 'Corner' held a vigil. Nearly the entire population of Webster attended the candle light service. The table Cindy and Debbie had sat at so many Friday afternoons was covered with mementos.

The two beloved teachers had been killed in a tragic accident. Apparently, a truck driver with a history of alcohol fueled anger was thrown out of a strip club for fondling the dancers. Instead of quietly going into the night he went back to his truck and got a gun. When he tried to reenter the club the bouncer attempted to stop him. A wrestling match ensued, then the fight escalated to where shots were fired. When police arrived they found the bouncer on the sidewalk. He had been shot in the stomach and was fading fast.

However, the shooter and his truck were missing. That is until one of the officers looked across the quiet tree lined street. "Holy crap," was all he was able to mutter as he surveyed the carnage. The 18 wheeler had accelerated across the street, its driver dead at the wheel. The big truck had crashed into the side of an abandoned building. Crushed under its wheels were the mangled bodies of two women, sisters, who happened to have been walking back to their hotel room after eating a quiet dinner in a restaurant that had reminded them of a certain deli in New Jersey.

The courts ruled Cindy died first thus her estate went to her older sister. Debbie had never changed her life insurance policy after her divorce. In a very ironic turn of events Debbie's estate went to her ex-husband. Today Roger and his 22 year old whore Maria very much enjoy riding their nearly new Harley-Davidsons 883's.

I'm Just A Man

Something was kicking my butt. I was as sick as a dog. Whatever it was, it was raising havoc with my stomach. Twice I had to stop and spill my guts by the side of the road. To make matters worse one minute I was hot and sweating profusely the next minute I was covered in goose bumps and freezing. I truly felt like crap, but for reasons I can't explain, I rode on.

Finally after a half hearted attempt at downing a Big Mac I saw the light and called it quits. At a few minutes past one on a beautiful June day I duck walked my sportster to the space in front of room 17 of the Sunset Hotel.

I quickly unpacked the duffel bag from the sissy bar, went into the room and turned the AC on full blast. Then, too tired to even take off my boots, I fell into the bed. Within minutes I was fast asleep.

I woke up with a start. From outside my room came the faint sound of a motor idling and people talking. Was my bike being ripped off? I jumped out of bed and rushed to the door. I opened it and was nearly blinded by the light.

When my eyes adjusted to the light I saw a guy and a girl standing on the walkway in front of the next room. Each held a can of beer. In the parking space in front of them a ratty shovelhead idled. The seventy-four had definitely seen better days.

Noticing me the girl gave a friendly wave. "How you doing?" She asked with a broad smile.

"I've been better," I answered after a pause.

"Want a beer?" she offered as she hoisted the can she was holding.

I chuckled. "No thanks. I think that is what got me in the shape I'm in." Again she smiled. Then she shrugged her shoulders. I could be wrong; however, she appeared too young to drink. With her soft and unblemished skin, golden blonde hair and cute figure I'd guess she was no more than 17 years old. In my mind she was the very picture of a sweet and innocent teenager.

Her male friend was another case entirely. From behind her he turned and spat into the parking lot. Then he glanced at my sportster. "Your bike?" he asked with a sneer. Before I could answer he went to his Harley and shut it off.

"Yeah," I answered as he pocketed the key to his ratty FL, "it's my bike."

He glanced at my XL before again turning his focus to me. For a long moment we just looked at each other, studying the other man. As he was wearing sunglasses and his face was covered with jet black hair I could only guess at his age. I ventured him to be in his thirties. But that was only a guess.

"I had a sportster once," he said slow and deliberate. "Then I grew up and got a real motorcycle." He laughed. His contempt was palatable.

When he stopped laughing I bore into him. "That's funny. I once had an AMF bowling ball bike then I grew up and bought a Harley-Davidson."

With that said I went and sat on my bike. He walked back to the girl. "Get inside," he commanded as he grabbed her by the elbow. Their door slammed shut.

After a couple of minutes I went into the room and got my cleaning supplies and rags. I was wiping the wax off the tear drop gas tank when their door opened. Out stepped the guy. In one fluid motion he got on, righted then started his bike. Glancing over his shoulder he called to the girl. "Hurry up. And don't forget your key." From inside the room the female answered, "I'm hurrying."

When she stepped onto the sidewalk I nearly did a double take. Though I had only seen her for a couple of minutes she had most definitely changed. Whereas earlier she had been dressed in jeans and a long sleeve button down blouse she now wore a halter top, a short skirt and high heels. The girl who I had thought was 17 still looked young but no longer did she look sweet and innocent.

As she climbed on the back seat of the motorcycle the guy turned to me. "Fuck you." He snarled. Then he revved the engine and took off. I watched the black FL shoot across the parking lot. Then in a roar of drag pipes the Harley entered the evenings' rush hour traffic.

Suddenly I was hungry. Fortunately, directly across the street from the hotel was a steak house. However, before I could eat I needed to get myself presentable. I gathered up my cleaning items and went into the room. I showered and changed into clean clothes. While combing my hair I could not help but notice how much better I felt. Whatever had been bothering me had passed.

As I closed the hotel room door I glanced at the clock on the night stand. It was exactly six.

Inside the restaurant there was a line of customers waiting at the cash register. A little white haired woman about 100 years old was taking their orders and ringing them up. From the speed with which she took the money and made change it was conceivable that she was being paid by the decade. She was working as slowly as humanly possible.

As I stood there my mind went back to the summer I turned eight. My mother had taken me clothes shopping; not exactly what any boy wants to do. However, mom knew how to get me to behave. She bribed me. "If you are good I'll buy us milk shakes," she promised. I behaved.

When we took our seats in the restaurant I was surprised to see my grand ma standing besides our table. She was wearing an apron and in her hands were a pencil and pad. It took me a moment to realize that she wasn't there to join us. Grand ma was a waitress. Years later I learned that if not for the tips she made at the diner she could not have paid her bills.

"What would you like to drink with your meal?" The elderly cashier asked snapping me back to the present.

"Coke, please." I answered.

"That will be $13.95." She said robotically.

I took out two tens from my wallet. As I handed them to her I read her name tag.

"Ruth you can keep the change." I took my receipt and walked into the dining room.

I pretty much keep to myself. I have more then enough trouble running my life to start running other peoples' lives. Still I could not help but wonder what kind of relationship the couple at the hotel had. She was young, pretty and friendly. He was older, rough looking and an asshole. As my friend Charles would say 'something doesn't seem kosher." Whatever the answer, it would have to wait till after dinner. I was hungry and there was food in front of me.

The sun had just set when I trotted across the highway to my hotel room. My XL1200 had company, the ratty shovel was back in its' spot. And its' owner was in the doorway smoking a cigarette.

Neither of us said a word as I walked past the two bikes to my room. When I got inside I closed the door. Not a minute later I was brushing my teeth when I heard the shovel come to life. With tooth brush in hand I opened the door. The FL was gone.

On my way back to the bathroom I stopped and turned the television on. I flipped from one channel to another looking for something intelligent or funny to watch. I didn't linger long in front of the set. "Crap. Screw it." I remarked aloud. I finished brushing my teeth then grabbed my helmet and key. I was going for a ride.

It felt good to be back on the sportster. After a week and a half on the road the XL's seat felt as comfortable to my rear as did my couch back home.

My ride around town didn't last very long. Other than two or three blocks of hotels and restaurants there wasn't much to it that I could find. And I looked. I quickly concluded that this was no more than a rest stop for travelers on the interstate. This was no ones destination.

Somewhat let down I decided to return to the hotel. Maybe, I thought to myself, there was a movie on the tube worth watching. However, before calling it a night I needed to go to the bathroom. I steered the 1200 into a fast food restaurant's parking lot.

The pretty blonde from the hotel was in a booth by the door. With her was a guy, who like her biker friend, appeared much older then her. They appeared to be discussing something important.

I hadn't taken two steps when she recognized me. "Oh hi there neighbor," she called in as friendly a voice as ever heard. "Hello neighbor," I answered. Without breaking stride I went into the men's room.

I was drying my hands when he entered the bathroom. He immediately confronted me.

"You a cop?" he demanded.

I took a step back. "Get out of my face." I spat back.

"You a cop? Yes or no?" He inched ever closer to me.

I crumpled up the paper towel I had dried my hands with. "Listen stud, I don't know who you are but I'm walking out of here." I tossed the paper towel into the trash can and opened the door. However, I did not walk through it. He grabbed me by the shoulder. "You didn't answer me," he growled.

Reflexively I turned and kneed him in the groin. His grip on my shoulder tightened then relaxed as I kneed him a second time. He dropped to his knees with a groan.

The young blonde was still sitting in the booth when I walked through the door. Seeing me she jumped to her feet. "Where is he?" she asked.

"He's resting." I told her with a smirk.

Her pretty face was blank. "Resting?" She asked.

Just then the bathroom door opened. Seeing me the guy stopped in his tracks. "Come on out," I told him. He was hesitant. "It's over." I assured him. The guy carefully made his way past me. The girl and I watched as he got into his car and drove away.

I took in a deep breath of air. Then I slowly let it. "Now," I said turning my attention to the young lady by my side, "what just happened?"

Her answer surprised me. "What just happened?" she repeated. "Well let me tell you what just happened. You just cost me fifty dollars. And probably a beating."

Now it was my turn to have a blank expression on my face. Before I could respond she went around me and opened the door. I watched her sashay across the parking lot that separated the restaurant from a hotel.

"Well I'll be," I muttered under my breath, "she's a lady of the evening."

As I said earlier I pretty much keep to myself. What people do with their lives is their business. If that blonde wants to be a prostitute so be it. I went to my sportster.

I was about to insert the key when an all too familiar ratty shovelhead rode past the restaurant. I watched as it turned into the driveway of the hotel the blonde was walking to. The Harley stopped in front of the girl.

I pocketed the key. Though I could not hear what was being said it was clear they were arguing. The blonde held her ground, that is, until the biker got off the bike. Then it appeared that all the fight went out of her. Still that did not stop the guy from grabbing her with one hand and slapping her with the other. Once, twice, three times he slapped her. That did it.

"Hey asshole," I shouted as I strode across the parking lot.

He was still holding her when I reached them.

Seeing me he snarled, "Get the fuck out of here!"

"Let the girl go," I demanded.

The biker yanked the girl to him. "You want her? Fifty bucks."

I reached for my wallet; took out two twenties and a ten. "Let her go." I handed him the money.

He released the girl. "Go to him," he commanded. She didn't move. "Go to him," he repeated. Turning to me he shook his head. "Dumb whore." The blonde stepped closer to me. I put my arm around her.

"You two make a lovely couple," he laughed. Then he spat and went to his bike. "Now go fuck her. The clock's running. You got half an hour. I'll be back." He called as he brought the Harley to life.

"We're in room four," she said. Her voice was filled with resignation.

"We're not going to room four," I stated.

She turned to me. "Don't you want to fuck me?" she asked.

I hesitated for a moment as I tried to find the right words. "No. I do not want to fuck you. And most definitely not under these circumstances."

"Under what circumstances do you want to fuck me?" she shot back.

Again I tried to find the right words. However, all I could come out with was a question of my own. "How old are you? Sixteen, seventeen?"

The girl chuckled. Then laughed. "Sixteen, seventeen?" she repeated. "I'm twenty two. I'll be twenty three next month. The fifth."

When she saw that I did not believe her she continued. "I'll prove it." She opened her purse and took out her wallet. "Here," she stated as she thrust her drivers license in my face. The card looked legitimate and the date of birth did make her twenty two. I said the first words that came to mind. "I'll be."

"Now do you want to fuck me?" She asked. "Or would you rather I suck your dick?"

As tempting as both options were I hesitated. "How did you get hooked up with him?"

She was about to answer when I said; "Cindy."

She looked at me with incredulity on her face.

"I read your license." I explained.

For the first time since she waved to me inside the restaurant Cindy smiled. "You're a quick reader," she commented.

I nodded. "So how did a twenty two year old girl from Youngstown, Ohio get hooked up with a guy like him?"

Again Cindy smiled. "Wow. You are good." Then after a long pause she told me the story. It started almost a year ago. She had a job and an apartment. Life was pretty good. Cindy also was doing a lot of drugs. "Nothing addictive, mostly dope." When she lost her job she did not lose her drug habit. She got deeper and deeper into debt with her pusher. "George, that's his name, was my supplier. If you haven't noticed he's a member of a motorcycle gang. He let me get so far over my head that there was only one way he said that I could work it off. So here I am."

When I asked her how much money she owed Cindy whistled. "Sixteen thousand big ones."

"Minus fifty," I quickly pointed out.

Cindy shook her head. "If only that were true," she said sadly. "George gets half."

"What would you rather be doing?"

"What do you mean by that?"

"You had a job. What were you doing?" I inquired.

Cindy laughed. "You're not going to believe this but I worked in a GM factory. I was an assembly line worker."

"Why wouldn't I believe you," I teased. "Isn't it always like that? If you want to find a good looking woman go to a factory."

Again Cindy smiled. "And what do you do?"

"Well I don't own a GM factory so I can't give you back your old job. Sorry. However, I am a teacher. I teach American History to bored high school students. The kids say I'm the best remedy for insomnia in the world."

This brought a grin to the blondes' pretty face. Then there was silence. For a minute or two neither of us spoke. Finally Cindy spoke. And when she did her voice was soft and inviting, like that of a lover talking to her lover.

"Do you want to fuck me now?"

I rubbed my nose. "Only if you want to," I answered. Then quickly added; "Do you want to continue this life?"

"Hell no," Cindy snapped

I looked the pretty blonde in the face. "Have you thought of going to the police?"

My question elicited a laugh from Cindy. "Why of course," she sneered. "Officer, I'm a whore and I don't want to work for my pimp anymore."

"I'm sorry for asking such a stupid question."

Cindy responded by touching my hand. "I'm sorry too."

"What about leaving? Move in with a friend or relative?"

Before answering Cindy wiped a strand of her blonde hair that had fallen across her face. "My parents and I don't talk. They're dead." She paused a moment to gather her thoughts. "And my friends are just as bad off as me. Youngstown is a dead town. The only friend I know who got away clean married a soldier."

I nodded as I digested Cindy's plight. Then it came to me. "I have an idea," I began.

Now those of you who think I told Cindy that together we would confront George and then ride away together are wrong. I am not a knight in shinny armor riding a white horse going around rescuing damsels in distress. And those thinking I offered to pay off Cindy's debt, think again. I am a first year teacher not a corporate CEO. No, my idea was baser than either of those two ideas.

"Cindy," I said softly, "let's go fuck."

George was true to his word. Thirty minutes after he left Cindy and me in the parking lot he returned. He didn't waste any time.

"Open up," he demanded as he banged on the door. The door opened and Cindy appeared. They talked briefly then he went inside. When the door closed I started my sportster. I had a nice night for a ride, I thought to myself. I'll go back to the hotel and pack my things. Then I'm riding and I'm not stopping till I pull into my driveway.

It's in the blood

Brian reasoned that it had to be at least a hundred degrees. The whole country was suffering through a massive heat wave. When the lanky biker rolled out of Watsonville four days ago it was eighty seven and that was at five in the morning! A trucker in Nebraska called it 'the dog days of summer.' Brian called it miserafuckenable. He could not believe how crappy, dirty and tired he felt.

The sweat stained denim clad biker surveyed his surroundings, watched the heat shimmer off the convenience stores parking lot. He took a deep breath, finished off the bottle of iced-T he had been rubbing against his forehead. Then he burped which brought a smile to his tanned face.

The ride east had been a test of endurance for both Brian and his scooter. More than a few times he had to pull under an overpass so the shovelhead could cool down. Even with its oil cooler and a fresh batch of Harley's finest every thousand miles the big twin had suffered. Brian had suffered, too. At gas stops he would seek out the air conditioned buildings. Once inside he'd drink as much liquid as possible. However, it didn't matter. Ten minutes after getting back on the black top he would be as hot and as miserable as before. Still, he knew he had to continue.

Brian tossed the empty iced tea bottle into the trash can, walked slowly to his faithful low rider. He squatted next to the bloodstone red Harley. "Not much further," he said softly as he put the key in the ignition. Then he sat on the split seat. It felt good. Comfortable. Like he had been sitting on it for an eternity. Brian turned to take his spray painted white half helmet off the sissy bar but before he could a drop of sweat stung his eye. Brian grimaced then cursed as he rubbed the culprit with his fist. Not completely satisfied, he blinked his eyes rapidly then leaned forward. Tied to the handlebars was a once bright red bandana now faded and torn. Brian had tied it there the day he bought his pride and joy. That was more than 25 years ago when he was living in Arizona. The dealer had offered him a free T-shirt, but Brian had declined. "I got all the Harley T's I'll ever need," he remarked. What he didn't have was a bandana. The bright red one on the lady mannequin by the door had caught his eye. "I'll take that instead," Brian told the old man as he pointed to the bandana. Now all these years and near countless miles later he used that bandana to wipe the sweat from his face.

Brian sat on the bike a moment. Then he righted it, kicked back the stand. Again in a whisper he talked to his trusty steed. "We're almost there. About 300 more miles." The biker was tired. Four days and twenty eight hundred miles in this miserable heat had drained him. Drained him like an alcoholic drains a bottle. To the last drop. Brian drew in a deep breath, grabbed his helmet and strapped it on his sweaty head. Then he fired the shovelhead to life, shifted into gear and rumbled through the parking lot onto the city street. A block away was an on ramp to the interstate. The interstate that was taking him to a place he used to call home. Back to Paramus after all those years living life as a nomad. Brian opened the throttle. Eighty cubic inches of V-twin power pulled strong. In a flash of chrome and noise bike and biker roared onto the super slab.

The sun had long set when Brian reached his destination. He rolled slowly through the parking lot. So slowly that a quick glance at the tachometer showed the engine to be turning only a few R's more than at idle. Brian could feel every power pulse of the motor as he made his way to the steps of the 'Thief of Baghdad.' When the front Goodyear touched the steps Brian shut off the mill, put down the stand, stretched and yawned. For a moment he closed his eyes. He was so tired he could easily have fallen asleep on the seat. However, Brian would not let himself rest until he knew the answer. The answer to the question that had driven him relentlessly from one end of the continent to the other. The answer that was now only on the other side of a door.

"Get up buddy," Brian commanded, snapping himself out of his reverie. With new found energy he entered the bar. It took him a moment for his eyes to adjust to the darkened room. Once able to see he looked it over. Even on a good night the 'The Thief' wasn't crowed and tonight wasn't a good night. Less than a dozen patrons were in the bar. At a booth near the pool table sat a man and a woman. The woman Brian had come to see.

Brian strode over to the booth. Neither person noticed him until he slid in besides the attractive blonde. "Hello sis," he said to the surprised woman. "Brian!" she exclaimed, throwing her arms around her older brother's neck. For a long time they hugged. It felt good holding his sister again, Brian thought. It had been too long since the last time they had embraced. More than three years. Brian remembered that day well. It was her wedding day. He could still picture her that June day. She was beautiful, the All American girl. She had long blonde hair, a great figure and a smile that could light up a room. Though it had been difficult Brian had stopped thinking of Linda as his kid sister. She was a married woman. A married woman who Brian loved and cared a great deal about. The longer they held each other the more Brian had to fight to control his anger. If what he had heard was true someone was going to get hurt. And Brian was going to do the hurting.

Roy put down his beer. "What brings you back?' he asked in a bored voice. Brian looked his brother-in-law straight in the face. Brain had never liked him. Accepted him, yes, but never liked him. There was something shifty about the guy who had married his sister. What Linda saw in Roy was beyond him. Brian paused, turned to his sister. "Linda," he answered, "she brought me back." And she had. It was not that she had called or written to Brian asking him to pay a visit. In fact Linda had no idea that he was coming until he sat down besides her. It was Barbara, Linda's closest friend, who had started Brian on his long journey. A week ago Barbara had mailed him a letter. "Brian, I hope this isn't true, but I think it is. Linda is having trouble with Roy. I'm pretty certain that he is beating her." That last statement stopped Brian in his tracks. He could not understand or tolerate a man striking a woman. The anger welled up inside him. The thought of Roy hitting Linda got his blood boiling. "The bastard," he snarled through clenched teeth. Barbara closed her letter with a plea. "I don't know what to do. I've tried talking with her, telling her to seek help, but she won't listen. I was hoping you could call her and talk with her. Maybe she'll listen to you. Thanks, Barbara."

Brian vowed he would do more than just call and talk with Linda. This required a visit. Face to face. Brian put the letter down and immediately went into his garage. An hour later, the bike was packed, its oil changed, new plugs installed and the chain lubed. When he finished Brian made three phone calls. The first was to his business partner Steve. "I got to take care of some crap back east. Important crap. I'll see you when it's taken care of," he told his fellow carpenter. Then Brian called Arlene. Although they had just started dating things were moving along nicely. "Why don't you fly?" she asked. Brian laughed. "Young lady you have so much to learn about me. Rule number one, this boy does not fly. Period," he explained. "Well call me when you get back," she said. "I certainly will," he promised. Brian's final call was to Barbara. She was surprised to hear from Brian. "I'm coming out. I'll be leaving tomorrow morning. I should get there late Friday night," he informed her. "In that case," Barbara replied, "you'll find Linda and Roy at 'The Thief.' I sometimes think they live there." Brian said he knew the place. "That'll be my first stop." There was silence. "Well, I don't want to run up your phone bill," Barbara said with a laugh. "That's okay," Brian stated. They talked for a few minutes, mostly about life in general before saying good bye. "Thanks. Thanks a lot for your letter," Brian told Barbara. He paused a moment then continued. "I know Linda and I aren't the closest but she'll always be my sister. And I'll always be there for her." With that they hung up.

During the ride east Brian had given a great deal of thought to how he would handle the situation. Should he confront Roy? Should he just beat the crap out of him? Would threatening to beat the crap out of him if he ever laid a hand on Linda again do the trick? Or should he take Linda aside and listen to what she had to say? Ask if there was anything he could do? And more than once Brian wondered why he was even going. Linda hadn't asked for his help. Not that she would. Linda had always been self reliant and capable of taking care of herself. If things were actually as bad as Barbara said they were Linda would have left Roy. Or would she? That's a tough call. A decision Brian had to make for himself not too long ago. It's hard to walk out on a marriage. Even one as screwed up as his had been. Eight years or three years it's not as easy thing to do. But, he had done it. Now he hoped that if it were best for Linda to end her marriage she too would have the courage to do so.

When the waitress came to the table Brian ordered a soda. "Beer too strong for you?" Roy chided. Before Brian could answer Linda spoke up. "Let him drink what he wants," she said with a laugh, "he's a big boy." Roy grabbed her by the wrist, turning her in his direction. "You speaking for your brother now?" he growled. Linda was silent. "Well. Are you?" Roy demanded, his voice rising. "Honey you're hurting me," Linda said as she tried to free her hand. Roy squeezed her wrist tighter. Then he looked past her, right at Brian. "I'll let go of you all right," he said with a sneer on his pasty white face, "when I'm good and ready." With that said Roy released his wife's arm. It was obvious Roy had enjoyed showing Brian that he controlled Linda.

The three of them sat in silence as the waitress returned with Brian' soda. "Put it on my tab honey," Roy told her with a wink. Brian intentionally ignored Roy as he hoisted the glass. Just before he took a sip he turned to his sister. "How's that job at the medical office coming along?"

Linda let out a laugh. "It's fine," she said with animation. "I really like my job a lot."

"She brings home good money," Roy interjected as he signaled the waitress for a refill of his beer. "Real good money," he added.

Linda continued talking about her work as a billings clerk when she stopped. A second later she smiled and laughed.

"What's so funny?" Brian asked.

Linda remarked that a young doctor had a crush on her. "He's cute. Maybe he'll ask me to his prom." She said it as a joke. However, Roy didn't laugh. Instead he snarled at Linda. "Yeah, you'd like that wouldn't you." Linda turned to him the smile still on her face. "I'm only kidding," she told her husband. Roy just starred at Linda. Brian could easily read his face. The man was on the verge of losing it. Linda knew it too. In a soothing voice she told Roy, "He didn't ask me," she teased, "because he had already asked Cindy Lou to the prom and she said yes."

"Bitch," Roy snarled. Linda was speechless. She started to speak when Roy backhanded her. Then he struck her a second time.

Instantly all of Brian's inner turmoil vanished. He knew what he had to do. In a flash he was out of the booth standing over Roy. Roy turned to him with a look of impunity. The seated man started to say something but before he could Brian delivered two lightning fast punches to his smug face. Then Brian grabbed the stunned man by the collar and hoisted him to his feet. "How does it feel?" Brian roared. "You like hurting my sister?" The visibly shaken man shook his head side to side. A thin stream of blood trickled out of his nose and down his face. Brian pulled Roy's face to within inches of his own. Then in a slow and very controlled voice he stated, "If you ever hurt my sister again I'll hurt you. Bad. Then I'll have you locked up. Do you understand?" Roy nodded his head in agreement. Brian let out a deep breath. Then he released Roy who slumped back in his seat.

"That's my husband you just hit!' Linda screamed at Brian. "Who are you to interfere in my life?" she demanded. Brian turned to his sister with a look of disbelief on his face. He was speechless. Then to add insult to injury Linda slapped his face. She then wet a napkin and began wiping the blood from Roy's face. Without looking up she called to her brother. "Why don't you get on your motorcycle and ride out of here?" For a moment Brian did not know what to do. Then he remembered something Barbara had told him over the phone. He reached out and took off Linda's sunglasses. Her left eye was nearly swollen shut and despite a heavy dose of make up it was still black and blue. "Nothing gave me the right," Brian stated, "if you want more of those." He handed her the shades. As he turned to leave the waitress came to the booth. The biker took a five from his wallet, dropped it on her plate, downed the soda and without a glance back walked out the door.

He started the low rider, shifted into gear and slowly released the clutch. He did not make it far before he pulled onto the shoulder of the road. He had to stop. He was so disgusted that he almost puked. The bastard had manhandled Linda right in front of him. And that black eye. No telling where else she was black and blue. Brian couldn't believe the way Linda had turned on him. She had acted as if he and not her husband had hit her. However, what angered him the most was the way she had knelt besides Roy and wiped his bloody nose, coddling him and calling him 'baby.' That was the last straw. If Linda was that stupid then she deserved whatever Roy gave her. Brian swore aloud never to get involved in his sisters life again. "She's too screwed up," he shouted into the night. Had he not been so tired he would have started back to California. Instead he checked into the first hotel he came across. After paying the desk clerk he rolled the Harley into the room. Then he spread out the complimentary copy of the Wall Street Journal under the crank case and final drive chain. "The perfect use for it," he remarked with a laugh. Exhausted he closed the door and turned out the light.

Brian slept late the following morning. He would have slept even longer had not the maid knocked on the door. "Come back later," he shouted. "Check out time is in half an hour," the faceless voice shot back. Brian looked at his watch. It was 11:32. Reluctantly he got out of bed, showered and dressed. As he packed his saddlebags his stomach growled. "I hear you loud and clear," he told his stomach. When he opened the door the maid was waiting for him. "You're the last room," she explained. Brian nodded, went back into the room. He picked up the oil stained papers, threw them into the waste paper basket. Then he slowly guided his bike through the door. The maid watched in amazement. "You kept that in your room last night?" she asked shaking her head. Brian gave her a puzzled look. "Kept what in the room?" he coyly asked. He put his helmet on and started the engine. "The keys on the bed," he called to the maid as she entered the room.

Brian rode to a highway diner he had eaten at many times before. An attractive teenage waitress showed him to his seat. "Would you like coffee?" she asked in a deep Jersey accent. "No thanks," he replied with a grin. It felt good to be home he thought to himself. The hungry biker picked up the menu. A few minutes later the waitress returned and took his order. While he waited for his meal he flipped through the pages of the table jukebox. There were a couple of songs he wanted to play, however, he didn't have any change. Getting up he went to the cashier. "I'd like to play the juke box," he informed the heavyset man behind the register. Brian opened his wallet and took out a single. Mindlessly the cashier handed him four quarters. Before Brian closed his wallet he took out a small crumpled piece of paper.

He looked at it for a moment then instead of returning to his seat he walked to the opposite end of the diner. He picked up the phone, deposited a quarter and dialed the number on the paper.

"Hello," answered a female voice.

"Barbara, this is Brian."

There was a pause. "Brian, it's good to hear from you. Did you just get in?"

"No," he stated, I got in last night." He then proceeded to tell her what happened at 'The Thief.'

Barbara listened intently. When Brian finished she spoke up. "What are you going to do now?" She sounded worried.

Brian let out a whistle. His stomach growled. "How about this," he began, "I'm at the Good Morning Diner on 17 and my breakfast should be on the table. I'm going to eat and then I'm going to get on my bike and head home. Back to California." He would have ended the conversation then, however, something told him not to.

"Don't leave. I'll be there in 15 minutes." Barbara said hurriedly.

Barbara was true to her word. Fifteen minutes later she entered the diner. Brian stood up to greet her.

For more than half an hour they discussed what to do about Linda and Roy. Finally, Barbara suggested she call Linda on her cell phone. Brian agreed, saying it was a good idea. They left the diner and went to Barbara's Ranger. She started the truck and immediately turned on the air conditioner. "Damn, that feels good," Brian remarked with a look of satisfaction on his face.

"You mean your bike doesn't have AC?" Barbara asked with a smile.

Brian returned the smile. "It has AC, but only in the winter. In the summer the heater won't shut off."

Barbara laughed, then she opened her purse. "There you are," she announced when she pulled out her cell phone. As Barbara punched in Linda's number she muttered, "I hope she's home."

Linda was home. "Hey friend," Barbara began in a very jovial voice, "how are you?" Linda talked with Barbara but balked when Barbara suggested she speak with her brother.

Linda was adamant. "Not after what he did to my husband last night."

The two women talked some more. Barbara was blunt. "Roy is going to hurt you. He'll hit you again and again until you leave him. He's not going to stop." She stated very forcibly. Then Barbara pleaded for her to get of her apartment. "You can stay with me."

Linda laughed, then confidently answered, "Roy's not going to hurt me anymore. He promised." Barbara did not have to repeat what Linda said, Brian heard her every word.

Brian couldn't stand it any longer. He took the phone from Barbara.

"Linda just listen," he began, "I love you and will do anything you ask. If you want my help just say so and I'll be there. But you gotta leave Roy."

There was a moment of silence. A glimmer of hope came across Brian's face. It was quickly shattered.

"My big brother rides all the way cross country for his little sister. And why did he do that? So he could butt into her life, that's why."

Brian shook his head in disbelief. He handed the phone back to Linda, grabbed his helmet.

"I'm out of here." He opened the trucks' door, but stopped when Barbara grabbed him by the arm. Don't leave," she pleaded in a voice barely audible. Brian closed the door. Barbara spoke into the phone.

The conversation ended a minute or two later when Linda abruptly said she had to go.

"Well what do you think?" Barbara asked as she put the phone back in her purse.

The biker took a deep breath then slowly let it out. "She sounds delusional."

Barbara nodded in agreement. "Yeah, she's in denial all right. She can't admit to anybody that her husband hits her. Linda the great success story couldn't have married a wife beater."

For what seemed an eternity neither person spoke. They just sat there with the cool air blowing over them.

Barbara broke the silence. "What are you going to do?" she asked as she turned the AC control knob down a level.

Brian didn't answer. He was lost in thought, thinking things through.

"Are you going back to California?"

Brian continued to stare into space.

Silence returned to the Ford. A minute, perhaps two passed before Brian spoke.

"Yes," he began, "I'm going back to California."

Barbara nodded her head ever so slightly. It was the answer she had expected to hear.

She was about to say something when Brian continued.

"I'll start for home in a couple of days. But for now my place is here. My kid sister needs me, whether she knows it or not. And I'm staying."

Linda could hardly contain her excitement. "You're a good brother," she blurted out.

"I'm also a brother," Brian said with a grin, "who is dead on his feet and has a sore ass."

Linda laughed as she brushed back a strand of hair that had fallen on her nose. "Where will you stay?" She wondered.

Brian had always gone for broke. 'If you don't ask the question,' he once explained to a friend, 'you'll never know the answer.'

The biker turned to Barbara. "Where will I stay?" he repeated. Barbara nodded her head. Brian looked her straight in the face. "With you of course," he stated.

Barbara was startled but not surprised. "Why don't you follow me home?" she asked with a smile.

"That sounds like a great idea," Brian remarked.

Brian followed the blue Ford to an apartment complex in a neighboring town. After they parked their vehicles they started to walk to her apartment. When they were a few steps from the door 'lady' began playing in Barbara's pocketbook. She stopped and took out her cell phone. "Hello."

"Barbara I'm just around the corner from your place. He hit me again." Linda was talking loud enough for Brian to hear.

Not two seconds later Linda's red Chevy pulled into the parking lot. Brian dropped his duffel bag and he and Linda ran to her. Linda screeched the car to a stop. Then she ran into the arms of her brother and her best friend. They hugged for what seemed a very long time but was probably only a minute or two. They might have hugged even longer had not one of Barbara's neighbors shouted, 'shit!'

The coroner's report would state that each was killed by a single shot to the head. Roy had always been a good shot.

Gray Dogs

It was early afternoon on a very hot August day. It was our third day on what appeared to be an endless ride. Like the two previous days Barb and I had started out long before the sun crested the horizon. We had a lot of miles to cover, Seattle to Bisbee. Much of it would be through the desert. Neither of us wanted to go through it in the middle of the day so we did our riding in the morning. Around noon we'd call it quits and get a hotel room. We didn't like the heat, nor did our low rider. Even with its oil cooler the 80-inch shovelhead often sounded like a rattlesnake had gotten inside it.

We had just crossed into the Grand Canyon State from Utah when Barb leaned over my right shoulder.

"You going to start looking for a hotel?" She asked.

I nodded in agreement. Satisfied, Barb leaned back against the pad on the sissy bar.

There were few exits on the state highway we were on and fewer signs of civilization. We were in the middle of the proverbial nowhere.

I leaned back. "Not the place you want to have a breakdown." I commented.

We rode on and the day got hotter. I dropped my left hand to the oil tank. It was too hot to touch for more than a second. "We'll call it a day soon." I said silently to my trusty friend.

As we crested a hill we saw the sign. A couple of the letters on it were missing, but two miles ahead was an exit for a town. That was good enough for me. "We'll see what this place has to offer." I called back to Barb. She rubbed my neck, her way of saying yes.

Two miles later I leaned the front Goodyear onto a beautiful sweeping off ramp. It had to be the longest and sweetest off ramp I had ever been on. Best of all, there was no stop sign at the bottom, so I rolled open the throttle and accelerated onto the country road. We followed the two-lane blacktop deeper into the desert. Mile after mile we rode. "If there's a town out here, it certainly is well hidden." Barb remarked. There was a hint of frustration in her voice. The heat was starting to get to her. I knew how she felt-I was starting to get pissed off too.

I took my left hand off the bar and placed it on her knee. "We'll find it." I assured her.

We found it. It was more a collection of dilapidated buildings than a town.

Barb sized it up immediately. "It's a town in name only." She stated. I agreed.

The semi-ghost town did have a gas station and a diner. They were across the nearly deserted main drag from each other. I stopped in front of the diner.

"Why don't you get us a table and I'll fill up the bike." I said, pointing to the gas station.

Barb looked across the street. "I wonder if it's even opened." She commented.

"I'll find out quick enough." I told her. Barb got off the bike and I rode the short distance to the lone pump. As I shut the bike off a gray dog woke up from in front of the office door. He took one look at me then trotted off around the corner of the building. "Sorry about disturbing your nap old boy." I called out after him.

A second later the attendant appeared from around the same corner of the building the gray dog had gone. He was tucking his work shirt into his pants. Spotting me he called "pump it yourself." He entered the office and I dismounted my bike.

Before I finished filling the two Fat Bob's the gas jockey joined me. He was tall and rail thin with greasy gray hair on top of which was a ratty ball hat. "Nice looking bike." He remarked.

"That it is," I stated as I took the nozzle out of the tank.

"What year is it?" He asked as he checked out my ride.

"It's brand new. An '81." I answered, placing the nozzle back in the pump. Then I got a twenty out of my wallet, handed it to him. He glanced at the bill. Whistled. "I'll have to get change in the office." He walked back to the building.

When he returned he counted out my change. "You're not from around here, are you?" It was more of a statement than a question. Still I gave him an answer. "No, I'm not from around here." I pocketed the money and hit the starter button for the ride across the street.

The diner was air-conditioned and it certainly felt good. Barb was the only customer, a fact that didn't escape her attention. The moment I sat down she leaned across the table. "Ten to one on a workday and the place is deserted." She whispered, barely holding back a laugh.

I smiled. "I was probably the only customer the gas station had all day."

We both laughed. Then we both took a long drink from the glasses of iced tea in front of us.

The instant Barb finished her glass of iced tea the waitress appeared and refilled it. "Thank you." Barb said. The matronly woman remarked that it was a hot one, then disappeared.

"She's a very good waitress." Barb remarked. "That's my third glass. Each time she filled it up within seconds of me finishing."

The cook was also good at his trade. Barb and I both commented on the hamburgers and fries. While we were eating something suddenly caught Barb's eye. "Look." She said, pointing to the gas station. I turned and looked out the window. I saw nothing unusual.

"You missed it." Barb said, still looking out the window.

"Missed what?" I wondered.

Barb turned to me. "A dog stood up and opened the door to the gas station."

I laughed. "A dog stood up and opened a door." I said in disbelief.

Instantly Barb snapped. "Yes, a dog stood up, opened the door and went inside."

I didn't know what to do, so I looked out the window. "Sure enough." I said. "I see a Fido."

Barb hurriedly turned her attention back to the gas station.

"That's the dog!" She said excitedly.

The dog was the one I had seen earlier, and he was doing exactly what he had been doing then; lying in front of the door sound asleep. I didn't know what to say, so I kept silent.

"You don't believe me." Barb said. Her voice was even toned.

I didn't answer. A long moment of silence followed. Then Barb started to laugh. "A dog standing up and opening a door!" She howled, laughing ever louder. Tears began flowing down her cheeks. I joined in; laughing to tears flowed down my cheeks.

"We've been in the sun too, too long!" I remarked.

Barb finally composed herself, nodded. "Woo! You're right. We've been in the sun too long."

We were still laughing softly when the waitress reappeared. "Would you like dessert?" She inquired. Barb and I looked at each other. "I couldn't eat another bite." Barb confessed. "Very good, food." I added. She handed me the bill. I quickly looked it over, took a five-dollar bill out of my wallet. Barb watched as I placed it on the table. "For the fine food and great entertainment." I joked.

Miracles never cease. There was a hotel in this one horse town. "It's a nice one, too." The waitress told us. And she was telling the truth.

The hotel was just a mile or so down the road. It was a large building, three floors tall and a city block long. There was not a car or truck in the parking lot, nor any signs of life. "Is it deserted?" I wondered aloud. Still we rode up its long driveway. Halfway up it, Barb let out a whistle. "Who would ever believe?"

I stopped the Harley in front of the hotel office. "Well, I'll be." I said in awe as I pocketed the key. In the shade of the building a gray dog was sleeping. He could have been the twin of the dog at the gas station. He woke up, looked at us, and then trotted off. Both Barb and I laughed.

"We have a way with dogs." Commented my erstwhile traveling companion. We walked into the office. The hotel clerk greeted us with a smile. "Welcome." He said. He was tall and quite thin. When we finished registering he summoned for a bellhop. One magically appeared from out of a hallway. "No need to," I protested, but in vain. The bellhop, another tall and thin man dutifully picked up our duffel bag and carried it to our room.

Our room, on the top floor, had a magnificent view. Off in the distance were purple and red and gold and blue mountains as far as the eye could see. The state highway we had traveled on was clearly visible as was the exit we had taken. We were able to follow the road we had ridden, first to town then to the hotel. Both Barb and I were surprised that neither of us had seen the hotel from the road. Perched atop a mountain as it was, one would expect that it would be visible from miles away.

Barb and I quickly changed into our bathing suits. We took the elevator to the first floor and followed the signs to the pool. It took us past the front desk. Out of the corner of my eye I caught sight of a gray dog. He had just gotten up and was ambling down a hallway. A moment later the clerk who had registered us came to the desk. Again, he greeted us with a smile. I commented about all the gray dogs I had seen. "The one who just ran off now, the one at the front door and the one at the gas station." The clerk chuckled. "I bet you would like to know about all them gray dogs." He stated with a Cheshire grin. Both Barb and I nodded in agreement. The clerk leaned across the counter. Then in a voice barely above a whisper he told us a story. It soon had us laughing out loud. It was also a story neither of us will soon forget.

It was a few minutes before four. Shift change at Mountain Top Hospital. Nurse Karen was briefing her relief, nurse Donna. They were in the room of a 25 year old man who was fast asleep.

"He and his girlfriend are lucky to be alive." Karen explained. "She's in room 305. Around noon they crashed their motorcycle in the desert. Fortunately," She added, "there was a truck driver behind them who saw the accident."

Donna picked up the chart at the end of the bed. While she studied it Karen continued. "Funny thing, the truck driver said the biker was going down the road fine, when suddenly he put on his turn signal. Then he leaned the bike as if he was exiting the highway. The only thing, there was no exit for miles. They crashed in a ditch just off the road. Had not the truck driver seen them they could have laid there for days"

"Indeed, they are lucky." Donna stated.

Karen nodded in agreement. "Besides some bruises, dehydration and heat exhaustion they're both going to be okay. Evidently, he passed out while driving his motorcycle."

"Not exactly the best place to pass out." Remarked Donna.

Karen smiled at her friend. "You're supposed to pass out on bar room floors or in living rooms. Not on a motorcycle going down the highway."

"How is his girlfriend?" Inquired Donna.

Again, Karen smiled. "Same as her beau. Evidently, she was already in la la land when he joined her. Neither knew what happened even when they woke up in the their rooms." The two nurses walked out the door and turned in the direction of room 305. Karen paused. "Mary from the ER said it was comical when they were brought in." She related with a laugh. "She said they were both unconscious but they were talking to each other."

"Unconscious and talking to each other?" Donna repeated with a hint of disbelief in her voice.

Karen nodded. "Yes, talking to each other. Mary said they were having a grand old conversation. And that they were laughing up a storm."

"I wonder what was so funny?" Asked Donna.

"Well," Continued Karen, "according to Mary the two of them were seeing gray dogs turn into people."

The two nurses laughed.

Old Photograph

This morning I happened upon a long forgotten photograph. It brought a smile to my face as I hadn't seen it in years. The picture was of a young couple sitting on a chopped sportster. Both are looking into the camera, however neither is smiling. In fact they both looked pissed, especially the pretty blonde on the back seat. I turned the photograph over and read: "Saturday April 21, 1973." I quickly did a little math in my head. "Thirty six years," I muttered in near disbelief. In spite of the passing of so much time I remember that day quite clearly. It was the day Cindy and I and our friends Husein and Mary rode to Washington, DC.

Cindy's dad was on the front lawn that morning when I parked the 900cc Harley at the curb. He was bent over the lawn mower with a screwdriver in hand.

"Morning Mr. J," I called as I took my helmet off. Cindy's father turned, acknowledged my presences, went back to fiddling with the lawn mower. He was not the friendliest guy in the world.

I walked past him and before I reached the steps Cindy opened the front door. She was smiling from ear to ear. "I'm so excited," she said, "we're going to Washington." From behind her came what Cindy and I called the voice of doom. "You better be careful with my daughter on that motorcycle of yours," sternly warned Cindy's mother. She was standing in the hallway.

"I'll be so careful," I promised her, "that I'll pretend that my life is at stake too."

Mrs. J. gave me a dirty look then went back into the kitchen. She was not the friendliest woman in the world.

I reached out and held Cindy's hands. "You look great." I told her. And she did. Cindy was of average height, but there was nothing else average about her. Dressed in skin tight jeans, a pink halter top and a denim jacket she was definitely a looker.

Just then the familiar sound of Hussein's 1000 could be heard. I glanced out the window; my friend was backing his XLCH next to my XLH. Mary was on the back seat leaning against the sissy bar. Her helmet was off and she was running a brush through her hair.

"We better get going," I said. Cindy hugged her mother while I grabbed my girlfriend's helmet. We went out the door.

Mr. J. was still working on the lawn mower as we walked past him. "So long dad," Cindy called to him. "It's supposed to rain this afternoon." Mr. J. stated without breaking stride or looking up. "It's coming from the south," he continued. Then he turned and faced us. "Washington, DC is south of here." Thinking back I could almost swear that there was the hint of a smile on his face.

We could not have picked a better morning for a motorcycle ride. The sky was robin egg blue and nearly cloudless and the sun was out in all its glory. The temperature seemed to rise with every rotation of the Goodyear tires. Within minutes I started unbuttoning my denim jacket.

Husein was in the next lane as we stopped to get our tickets for the pleasure of riding the New Jersey Turnpike. I handed Cindy our ticket which she neatly folder then put in her breast pocket. I pulled forward, looked to my left. Husein signaled that he was set. I nodded, brought in the clutch, tapped the shifter arm with my right foot. Our two Harley's accelerated into the fast moving melee that was the Turnpike.

Husein and I quickly worked our way into the far left lane. Once there we settled in at an indicated 70 miles per hour. Husein and Mary on his blue '72 were slightly ahead and to the left of Cindy and me on my red '71. As I stretched my feet to the highway pegs Cindy leaned back against the sissy bar. Blasting down the highway on your Harley with your girl behind you and your buddy and his girl on their Harley in the next lane, well life doesn't get much better. However, like all good things it had to end. Those iconic tear drop gas tanks needed gas. Our ride in the fast lane had lasted a whole ten minutes.

No sooner had the girls gotten off the bikes then trouble reared its ugly head. Mary's right pants leg was covered in oil! Husein quickly put two and two together. In anticipation of his upcoming cross country trip he had replaced the 21 tooth primary sprocket with a 23 tooth sprocket. The bigger sprocket would deliver better gas mileage. However, the bigger sprocket raised the chain just enough that it rubbed the oil tank causing a hairline crack.

While Mary and Cindy went to the ladies room to clean up Husein and I gassed the bikes then rolled them to an area where we could work on the 'CH. First thing Husein did was check the oil level. "It's fine," he said showing me the dip stick. Next he got out his wrenches from his tool bag. We quickly tightened the chain. "Now to fix the leak," Husein stated as we walked to the service bay. One of the mechanics gave us a glue tube, a tire patch and a clean rag. We completed the job in a couple of minutes. Seconds after I returned the borrowed items the two girls came out of the ladies room. In spite of having a pair of jeans ruined Mary was not upset.

After our unexpected mechanical delay it felt good to back on the road. Traffic was lighter the further south we traveled. The bikes were running like champs and the miles rolled by effortlessly. It wasn't long before Husein waved till he got my attention. He pointed down to his gas tank. I acknowledged his signal. Our second visit to a Turnpike service area that morning went better and quicker than our previous one. We were in and out in probably less than five minutes.

At the south end of the Turnpike the Delaware Memorial Bridge can be seen towering above all else. It is an impressive structure. It is long and it is high. From its apex you have an excellent view of the tri state area. Though I had ridden over it many times it was always with a certain sense of dread. And that had been in a car.

Cindy had never been over the DMB before. The moment she realized we would be crossing it she leaned forward. I fully expected her to express fear or at least anxiety. I was very surprised by what she said. "Get in the right lane," she urged me. There was a sense of excitement in her voice. "I want to see as much and as far as possible."

Against my better judgment I complied. By the time we reached the base of the bridge I had maneuvering us into the lane closest to the edge and eternity. Up we went, higher and higher. Cindy stood on the pegs, turned and looked in every direction. She was enthralled with the view. I dared not take my eyes off the road immediately in front of us. Cindy called out and pointed to the different sights. I hung onto the bars with a death like grip and silently cursed Cindy with all my being. When we successfully made it across I looked at Cindy in the mirror. She had an expression about her like that of a child at Christmas. I felt like I had run a marathon.

Riding I-95 in Delaware is a brief experience. One minute you're being welcomed into 'the state that started a nation' the next minute you're in Maryland. It was in Maryland that my hay fever acted up. I started sneezing. I couldn't stop, every minute a sneeze. My eyes watered and my nose dripped. I sneezed with all the fury of a mad man. And with every sneeze my face became redder and sweatier.

My uncontrollable sneezing did not go unnoticed. At first after every sneeze Cindy rubbed my shoulder and said 'God bless you.' That last about ten minutes, then she gave up. I sneezed so loud and so often that Husein and Mary heard me. They both looked over and smiled in anticipation of me sneezing. When I obliged they broke out laughing.

When we stopped for gas, yet again, at a rest area I was physically exhausted and close to being dehydrated. It took a long drink of water to replenish what I had sweated out. Funny thing though, after that stop I did not sneeze again!

The rest of the ride to DC was uneventful. We parked and locked the bikes and walked around the city. It felt good too stretch the legs after being on a bike so long. We were typical tourists. We climbed the stops to the Lincoln Memorial, walked along the reflecting pool and stood in front of the White House.

The four of us were about to leave when a White House employee appeared. He was dressed in the new uniform President Nixon had just mandated. I felt sorry for the guy, the uniform looked ridiculous. Cindy called and waved to him. She caught his attention. "Where's Dick?" Cindy shouted loud enough for half of DC to hear.

"The president," the employee called back in a very dignified voice, "is on vacation."

Without missing a beat Cindy called back even louder than before, "he's always on vacation.' The four of us busted up laughing.

It was while we were eating lunch that Mary mentioned it, the weather. "It looks like rain." Everyone turned and looked. "It sure does," Cindy stated. We quickly finished our hamburgers and started walking to the bikes. Less than a block from the two Harley's it started to rain. Not hard, not even a sprinkle. However, we all knew that it was a harbinger of things to come. We wasted no time, strapping on our helmets as we crossed the street.

Husein and I often joked about the advantages of our bikes. One of my bragging points about the XLH was its electric starter. Husein countered with his bikes bigger engine and lighter weight due to its lack of electric motor.

That day I knew three people who wished Husein had an electric start motorcycle. While my bike idled Cindy, Mary and I watched Husein valiantly attempt to start his bike. He finally got the 1000 started but by then we had lost the race against Mother Nature. It was drizzling.

We raced through DC and in a matter of minutes we were on the interstate. Our two Harley's roared as they took us north. It was a light drizzle and our denim jackets kept us dry. Then as suddenly as it started the rain stopped. Still we pressed on for a glance behind us showed a black mass over our nation's capitol.

The sportsters' Achilles Heel is its gas tank. Two and a quarter gallons of petrol get you less than a hundred miles under the best of circumstances. Running hard like we were they deliver even fewer miles. Seventy seven miles after filling up both bikes went on reserve.

The two bikers were topped off and we were back on the road in record time. We red lined through the gears. When we got to fourth I stretched my feet to the highway pegs. By the time we crossed the DMB and stopped for our Jersey Turnpike ticket it was evident, we had out run the storm. However, luck was not with us that fine spring day.

Less than half an hour's ride from home the biggest and blackest cloud I have ever seen appeared to our left. It just seemed to come out of nowhere, but, there it was and it was heading directly for us.

When it caught us there was no mistaking it. The rain came down in buckets. Our denim jackets were useless, we were instantly soaked to the skin. The wind blew and lightning bolts streaked across the sky. Everyone knows lightning strikes the tallest object. The section of the turnpike we were riding is elevated making us the tallest objects for miles! If I had been a bit nervous riding over the DMB I was now absolutely terrified. Cindy held on to me tighter than she had ever held onto me before. To say that it was a thrilling ride would be a gross understatement.

Cindy and I got off the turnpike one exit before Husein and Mary. When we stopped to pay our toll the guy inside the booth took our money then made a wiseass remark. I cannot remember what he said, but I do remember what Cindy said and what I did. My blonde companion told the guy to have sex with himself. Then I pulled forward a few feet, brought in the clutch and rolled open the throttle. I let the sporty's drag pipes scream. I'm quite certain that that toll taker went home with a headache.

The rain continued the entire distance to Cindy's house. It wasn't as hard as it had been on the turnpike but still hard enough to make for a miserable ride. We pulled into her driveway looking like drowned rats. We were beat.

I had just put the kick stand down when Mr. & Mrs. J came out of the house. Both were smiling. "Say cheese," they called in unison. Cindy and I just looked at them as Mr. J snapped our picture. That is the picture I found today. I suspect Cindy will get a laugh looking at it when she comes back from grocery shopping.

Midnight Rider

In the darkest hours, when the drunk is asleep and the mailman has yet to don his uniform, I ride. The midnight rider calls to me. It is red, black and chrome. Cleaned, polished and ready to ride. I fire it to life. Eighty cubic inches of shovelhead power thunders in the night. It roars like the king that it is. Nothing can catch my midnight rider.

We prowl the interstate. Looking for unsuspecting drivers. Cars or bikes. It doesn't matter. The midnight rider will take on all. They will look at the midnight rider. Some will snicker. The wiser ones will call for a roll on race. The foolish ones will agree to a standing start race. All will bet. Most will bet heavily. All will be humiliated. Vets, firebirds and mustangs. Jaguars and Porsches. Other Harleys and Jap bikes too. It doesn't matter. The midnight rider always wins. Always.

Before the first rays of light streak across the eastern skies the midnight rider and I are home. Tucked in our garage I check spark plugs, chain tightness, tire pressure, oil level and inspect the air filter. All are up to snuff. Then I lovingly clean and polish the midnight rider. Hour after hour. By noon I retire to my bed. When I awake it will be time once again to prowl the interstate.

It wasn't always like this. I once had a real life. A job. Friends. A wife. My wife Barbara and I had a good life together. She enjoyed an occasional putt on the low rider. A ride to the river. A ride to the mountains. Sometimes I took the bike to work. Like that day last June. It was a Friday. Pay day. After work a group of us stopped at a local bar for more than a few beers. It was our way of blowing off steam after a week of working on the assembly line. Mike and I were the last to call it quits. Mike mounted his sportster, fired it up and left in a cloud of burning rubber. Staggering to my bike I was suddenly confronted by him. He came out of the shadow. Even if I wasn't blitzed he would have looked out of place. In a neighborhood known for its bars and strip joints a guy in a tuxedo was a rarity. He introduced himself, but I quickly forgot his name. He started talking. I got on the bike, fiddled with the key, turned the petcock on. He continued to talk even as I started the low rider. "Would you like this to be the world's fastest motorcycle?" he asked gesturing to my idling bike. I nodded. "Sure." He smiled, produced a piece of paper and a pen. "Sign here and it will be," he assured me as he handed me the pen. I should have listened more closely to what he was saying. I certainly should have read what he held in front of me. But, I didn't. I was in a hurry to get on the road. I signed. "There," I said as I handed him the pen. He extended his hand. I grasped it. It was cold. Lifeless. This guy's a strange one I, thought to myself as I shifted into gear.

The low rider ran a lot stronger and crisper than usual. Must be the cool night air, I reasoned. Or the beer. Entering the interstate I opened the throttle. The bike pulled like never before. I glanced at the tach; the needle was past six thousand. I closed the throttle, shifted. No let up in power. Again a quick glance at the tach. Seven thousand and still climbing. Third gear. This time I tried to shift at around five grand. Couldn't do it. The crank was spinning seven G's when I put the FXS into fourth. I kept the throttle opened. The bike never stopped pulling. I glanced at the instruments. The speedo was buried and the tach was climbing past six thousand. Six thousand r's in fourth gear! I couldn't believe it. We must be doing a hundred thirty! I had never been able to do more than 115 before. Didn't think it was possible. I backed off the throttle. The tach needled drifted counter clockwise. When it crossed the four the speedometer needle came to life. I stopped it's descent at seventy five.

A moment later something else very strange happened. I flew past a cop car on the side of the road that had his radar gun aimed right at me. "Damn!" I muttered, expecting him to pull out after me. He didn't move. What was going on here? I wondered. I rode the rest of the way home in disbelief.

Monday morning I quit my job. The boss was surprised. "Twenty years down the drain," he said shaking his head. If he was surprised Barbara was shocked. She couldn't believe it. "How are we going to live?" she demanded to know. I couldn't answer her because I didn't know. Nor did I care. I stopped hanging around with my friends. I didn't need or miss them. I started spending all my time cleaning and polishing my midnight rider. And less and less time with Barbara. One night I woke up and found that she had left. "Call me when you remember who I am," she wrote in the note she had left on the seat of the midnight rider. My wife left me. It didn't matter. Nothing mattered. I had everything I needed. I had my midnight rider.

At first a lot of things seemed odd to me. Then I just accepted them. Things like, I never got hungry. Or thirsty. Or that I slept during the day and only came out at night. Or that I never got a second glance by any cop no matter what I did. Very strange. But, I wasn't about to complain. I had a new life.

The first time I got ready to race a crotch rocket I wondered if I was nuts. Those things are fast! I told myself as I walked around the ninja. The guy must have been thinking the same thing. When he looked at my pristine Harley he snickered. Then he gave me ten to one odds. My fifty dollar bill against his five C notes. He let me choose the race. "A roll on," I said. We started our bikes. His bike sounded nasty through his expensive high performance exhaust system. My bike sounded mute with its stock pipes. "To mile marker 15," he called as we shifted into gear. The two bikes rolled down the highway side by side at ten miles per hour. I dropped my left hand. The race was on. Both throttles were snapped back. The Kawasaki was fast. Very fast. Against most other bikes it would have been far out in front. However, he wasn't racing another bike. He was racing the midnight rider. The poor guy couldn't believe he had been beaten. Beaten by a Harley. And beaten badly. He got off his bike, went over to the midnight rider. Muttering incoherently he squatted next to it. He checked the engine from top to bottom. One side and then the other side. I watched him and I kept silent. I also kept his five hundred dollars. As he left I called to him. "Please, tell your friends." He did.

Night after night I raced against one bike after another. Performance bikes, turbo charged bikes, stroked bikes. Some raced from a standing start. Others from a roll on. Some chose a top end contest. It didn't matter. The midnight rider always won. I knew the midnight rider's fame was spreading; however, even I was surprised the night a Chevy van with California plates joined us. Out stepped three very tough looking dudes. "This is the Harley that's supposed to be so fast," one sneered at me after he glanced at the midnight rider. "How much money do you have to find out?" I asked with a smile. "Enough to buy ten of those slugs," he shot back. He and his friends laughed. When they finished I calmly stated, "Put your money where your mouth is." They did. Fifty big ones. I matched them with fifty thousand from my saddlebags.

"Since you're the visiting team I'll let you choose the race," I said. "Standing start half mile," came the reply. Without shaking hands the three men went to the back of their van. They opened the doors and put down a ramp. Then they rolled out one very slick looking multi colored Jap bike. I joined them. "Nice looking bike," I remarked. "Saw one just like it last week. In my mirror. It was going backwards." I laughed then walked over to the midnight rider.

Moments later we were on our idling bikes looking down an empty stretch of blacktop. "Anytime you're ready," I called to the Honda rider. He revved his engine. I yawned. We turned our attention to his friend who stood a few yards in front of us with his arms raised. The other rider and I nodded to him. He dropped his arms. The race was on. The west coast bike was fast. No doubt about that. It kept up with the midnight rider through most of first gear. I shifted into second. The Harley pulled strong. The midnight rider was getting up a head of steam. Third gear. The shovelhead screamed. Fourth gear. The midnight rider's power never let up. If anything it got stronger. In a flash the tach was buried yet again. I kept the throttle opened until I flew past the mile marker that signaled the end of the race. Only then did I shut the throttle down. The speedometer needle came to life as the Honda came along side me. I lead him back to his buddies.

They were smiling and laughing when we rolled to a stop. "How bad did you dust the dude?" one asked. The rider took off his helmet, shook his head. Then he let out a deep breath of air. He turned to his buddies. "He dusted me." Two mouths fell open.

For some unexplainable reason I didn't ride home immediately after the race. Instead I rode down a nearby country road. A nice tree lined curvy road. A road Barbara and I used to ride. That was when riding was fun. Relaxing. A lot more enjoyable than blasting down the interstate at warp speed. However, tonight it didn't feel right. No. It felt fine. It was me that didn't feel right. Something kept nagging at me. Pulling me in the direction of my house. A force. A very strong force. A very strong force that didn't want me riding to where I was headed. I rode on.

He was standing where I had first seen him. In the shadow of the bar. Barely visible. He was waiting for me, he knew I was coming. When I shut the midnight rider off he acknowledged my presence. He stepped out of the shadow. "I see you have been doing some racing," he remarked. I nodded. He continued. "You've made a lot of money." Again I nodded. He chuckled. "Surprised a lot of Jap bike riders." It was my turn to chuckle. Silence. "I take it," he said, "that you have something to tell me." I nodded as I stepped off the midnight rider. I walked up to him, looked him straight in the face. "I want my soul back," I stated as forcefully as I could. He smiled. He chuckled. He started to laugh. Then he roared. My face didn't change expression. Finally, he regained his composure. "You want your soul back?" he asked with incredulity in his voice. "Yes!" I shot back. "What makes you think I have your soul?" he answered coyly. "Because of the contract I signed," I stated, "and because you are the devil."

"Since I hold the contract," he said waving the piece of paper in front of me, "I should be the one who decides how you can void it." I was silent. "Good, we agree," he said. He paused a moment. "How can you void this legal and binding contract?" he asked softly. His face lit up. "I know," he called out gleefully. "We'll have a race. A motorcycle race. Your motorcycle against my motorcycle." He snapped his fingers. Instantly a Kawasaki dragster appeared. If ever a bike looked evil it was this one. It was solid black except for the red flames on the gas tank. But this was no ordinary flame job. This was different. The flames didn't go from the front to the rear of the gas tank. No, these flames went from the bottom to the top of the gas tank. Like the flames of hell. He turned to me with a grin on his face. I returned the gesture. "If you get to choose the means I should get to choose the course," I stated. "Of course," he readily answered.

He sat on his bike opening and closing the throttle. The roar was deafening. "A hell of a lot of power," he shouted with delight.

I ignored him. I was ready to press the start button when I stopped. Long ago Barbara and I had a tradition. Whenever we would go for a ride the first time I started the bike would be with the kick starter. I turned out the kicker, firmly planted my boot on the rubber. "Please start," I whispered to the eighty inch mill. It did. I gently opened the throttle. I instantly knew the super power was gone. Beneath me was a stock 1981 low rider. "Are you ready?" he called to me. "Yeah, I'm ready," I shouted back. "Here's the route we'll take. Down the interstate to the second exit. That's Charlestown Road. Take it north." I paused. "It's a windy road, so please be careful," I laughed. He didn't crack a smile. "Two miles or so," I continued, "the road splits. Take the left. That's Dreher Road. It's a short ugly road that T's with Worms Road." Again I paused. When I continued I spoke very slowly. This was my ace in the hole. "The winner is the first one in the parking lot on the corner." Before he could respond I shifted into gear and accelerated for the on ramp to the interstate. As quickly as I could I went through the gears. The shovelhead seemed to take forever to reach the interstate. When it did I checked the instruments. The tach was sweeping past three grand and the speedo needle was approaching seventy. And I was already in top gear! Before I could turn my attention back to the road a black bullet shooting flames shot past me. In less time than it took me to mutter, 'unholy shit,' his flames were but a speck in the night. I backed off the throttle; put my feet to the highway pegs. This was one ride I was going to enjoy.

He was exactly where I knew he would be; in front of the entrance to the parking lot that was our destination. And just as I expected the bike was snarling and he was fuming. With a small wave I rode past him and through the wrought iron gates into the parking lot of the Catholic Church where Barbara and I were married.

Cindy sleeps

It was unusual for Cindy to be awake at three thirty in the morning. The pretty blonde nurse normally was in bed by eleven, even on weekends. However, she had good reason not to be up stairs in her bed sound asleep. She was expecting her husband to walk through the front door any minute.

Mike had called around eight that evening saying he would be home as fast as his Harley would take him. A week earlier he had ridden to Florida for a wedding. Bad weather had compelled Mike to leave for home a day later than originally planned. That was the reason for him coming home so late. "Be careful," she had advised him, then she promised to wait up for him. "I'll like that," he stated as they hung up.

Hour after hour Cindy waited. She finished reading a book, wrote birthday cards to two nieces, and searched the internet for information on vacationing in Florida. Cindy had always wanted to swim in the ocean. She would have gone to the wedding with Mike if she had been able to get off from work.

By eleven o'clock Cindy was in her pajamas and curled up under a blanket on the couch. She reasoned that if she fell asleep she'd wake up when Mike rode his Harley into the garage. She did fall asleep, several times. Whenever a car rode past the house or a dog barked Cindy would sit up hoping that her husband of 12 years was home.

Around one Cindy turned on the television. When she finished flipping through every channel she laughed. "If people think there's nothing worth watching at night they should see what's on at one in the morning." Cindy settled on the eighties music channel. It was the music she grew up listening to. It was the music Mike and she had danced to when they dated. It was the music she most associated with Mike.

At two thirty Cindy went into the kitchen and made a snack. When she returned to the couch she was wide awake. She giggled at the thought of eating waffles smothered in chocolate ice cream and whipped cream at quarter till three in the morning.

Cindy was sound asleep when Mike opened the front door. For a moment he stood in the vestibule smiling at his inert wife. He quietly took off his boots then tip toed across the room to the couch. Just as he was about to kiss her forehead Cindy woke up.

"You're home!" she exclaimed as she wrapped her arms around his neck. They kissed.

"Let's go up stairs," Mike said as he helped his wife up from the couch. As they started to climb the stairs Mike took something from his pocket. He handed it to Cindy.

"Something for you," he told her.

Cindy looked at it with a puzzled expression on her face. "What is it?" she asked.

Mike smiled. "I know how much you wanted to swim in the ocean. But, since that was impossible, I got a little of the ocean for you."

Cindy studied the small glass container in her hands. She turned to Mike. "Thank you. That's the nicest gift I've ever got. I love you." They went up stairs.

At three thirty the door bell rang. It came to Cindy like in a dream. The bell rang again. Cindy sat up. She was surprised when she realized she had been sleeping on the couch. She walked to the door just as the door bell rang a third time.

Cindy was startled to see two policemen standing at her door. She was even more startled when they told her Mike had been killed in a traffic accident less than two miles from home.

"He can't be dead," she calmly informed the two policemen, "he's up stairs sleeping." Neither man spoke. Cindy started to gesture to the stairs but stopped when she saw the couch. For a second there was silence. Then Cindy realized the truth. "He can't be," Cindy softly muttered as tears began streaming down her face.

Cindy's sister Nancy lived across the street. She had looked out her bedroom window and saw the police car parked in front of Cindy's house. Sensing that something was wrong she threw on a coat and rushed to her sister's house.

The sun was rising when Nancy walked up the stairs with Cindy. Opening the bedroom door Nancy told Cindy "Sleep. We'll take care of everything." Nancy went to throw back the covers when she stopped. "What's this?" she asked.

Cindy looked at what Nancy held in her hand. It was a small glass container that held ocean water.

Cindy smiled, then she laughed. "It's a gift." Nancy nodded. Then Cindy added "Mike gave it to me this morning."

Sweet Dreams

American Motorcycle Repair and Service was the independent dealer that had been recommended to me by a fellow Harley rider. We were in a dive just over the Jersey-New York state line. I had told the biker about the crappy job the Harley dealer had done servicing my bike. "Not to worry," the man assured me. "Mike, the owner of AMRS, does good work and at half the price of the Harley dealer," the biker pointed out to me. I told him to go on. The heavy set man with a gold tooth and a tattoo of an eagle on his forearm continued. "He got my pan running better then it ran when it rolled out of the factory." Though I had no idea what a pan was I was nevertheless impressed.

The following afternoon I went looking for AMRS. After crossing what seemed like every railroad tracks in Bergen County I stumbled upon the place. Like the biker at the bar said the place was nondescript. Only the line of choppers out front distinguished it from the other decrepit building surrounding it. I backed the 900 to the curb.

I pushed open the wooden door and entered a world I had no idea existed. Two or three men stood at the counter, an equal number lounged about on over stuffed couches thumbing through magazines. Each, it appeared, held a can of beer. All were ragged looking. The air was filled with the sweet smell of pot and from two speakers came the music of a Doors LP. My first instinct was to bolt. However, I didn't.

"What can I help you with?" called the gray haired man behind the counter. I felt every eye boring down on me. I smiled. "I heard that Mike does good work on Harley's." I proclaimed in a voice far more confident then I felt. "And my Harley could use some good work." This brought a bear like laugh from the gray haired man. "Son," he said in a loud friendly voice, "I certainly hope that I do."

Mike had me roll my bike through the barn doors that opened to the work area. Inside two mechanics were working on bikes. One looked up from putting a tire on a tricked out 74. He acknowledged me with a nod then returned to the task at hand. The other guy was too busy studying the innards of a sporty transmission to pay me any heed. He wiped his hands on a rag, cursed, then like his fellow worker returned to the task at hand.

"Over there," Mike instructed me pointing to a spot near the tire rack. I dutifully rolled the white Harley to the far corner. "That's good," Mike called. I put the kick stand down.

Mike took a clip board from the wall. On the clipboard was a work order sheet. "Why don't you fill it out?" he said as he handed it to me. I took my time as I had a lot to say. When I finished Mike looked over what I had written. A smile appeared on his broad face. "It ran good," he read in his loud booming voice. The two mechanics stopped and listened. Mike continued. "That is until the so called mechanics at a dealership that will remain nameless got their hands on it. The bike spits, breaks up and does not run like the raped ape the HD mechanics promised that it would."

"Another screw up from our friends across the river," one of the mechanics stated in a voice equal to Mike's. The other mechanic quickly shot back. "Their customers are our best customers." Even I had to laugh.

Then I got the bad news. The bike would have to be left for at least two days. "We're backed up with work. And solid lifters can't be touched for 24 hours. They have to be dead cold before they can be adjusted," Mike explained. Then he quickly added with a friendly arm around my shoulder. "Why don't you relax and have a beer. We'll get you a ride home." It sounded like very good advice, so I gladly took it.

When we entered the waiting room Mike reached under the counter and opened a small refrigerator. He took out two Bud's.

"Here," he called as he tossed me a can. "Thanks," I shot back. With a cold beer in hand I took a seat on the couch by the door. Moments later I was reading a test report of Harley's newest bike, the super glide.

Her presence did not cause a stir. Not the slightest. Well, at least not in the other guys. However, she stirred me. I watched her every move as she walked across the room. When the slender blonde reached Mike she stopped. The two spoke briefly. "That's the guy," he informed her as he pointed to me. I stood up. "Her name is Cindy and she's my daughter. She'll drive you home." Mike stated in his booming voice. Cindy glanced at me then turned to her father. Everyone in the room could not help but hear what she said. "Are you sure he's old enough to be drinking?" And of course everyone laughed.

Cindy was all business. Even before we got in her car she had my address memorized. "That's off of Spring Valley, just past the school there," she remarked. Before I could confirm her directions she opened the door and slid behind the wheel. I started to speak when my words were drowned out by the roar of the Pontiacs engine. "Love the sound of a V8," she remarked. Then she quickly added, "almost as much as the sound of a V-twin." With that said the pretty lady gave it the gas.

The ride home was strange. It didn't bother me that Cindy drove. What struck me as odd was the fact that there was a complete lack of conversation. The couple of times I tried to elicit a response from Cindy were met with a cool indifference. I couldn't even get a hint of a smile from her. "Screw it," I thought to myself. I sat back and enjoyed the ride.

Without a word from me Cindy drove the exact route home that I would have taken. She even pulled into the driveway behind my dad's Buick. I opened the door and was about to get out when instead I turned to her. "Thank you. And by the way I am old enough to drink." I stepped out of the car and closed the door.

I hadn't taken two steps when she called. "Wait." I stopped in my tracks.

"Why don't you get back in the car?" Cindy asked with a smile.

I ran my hand through my hair, got back in the car. "What's up?" I countered.

Cindy turned off the ignition, turned in her seat to face me. Then almost pleading she blurted out, "I thought it couldn't be true. But I think it is." Not having the slightest idea what she was talking about I kept quiet. Cindy was quick to elaborate. However, her explanation did little to clarify what she meant. "I mean I was right about you."

For a moment it crossed my mind that Cindy was nuts. How could she be wrong or right about me, I wondered, when she knew nothing about me? I decided that at the count of ten I would simply thank her once again then get out of the car and walk into the house. I got to six when suddenly her flood gates opened. "This is going to sound crazy. Very crazy. Sometimes I can't believe it. But it's the truth." I leaned back in my seat and readied myself for what I suspected would be a memorable side trip into the world of a crazed person.

I wasn't disappointed. For ten minutes Cindy talked non-stop. At times she spoke so quickly that she became tongue tied. Other times she would pause for a second or two to gather her thoughts. Then it was back to the races. The tale she spun was the most unbelievable story I ever heard.

Cindy said the dreams began about a year ago. "I would have a dream one night and the next night it, the dream, would continue where the other had ended." At first she thought it was purely coincidental. "What are the chances of that happening?" she wondered.

"I started writing down my dreams," Cindy continued. "Each night before going to bed I would have a pen and pad handy. As soon as I woke up I would write down everything I could remember. The more I did it the more I could recall." Cindy got so good at remembering details that she started using a tape recorder. "I can speak a lot faster than I can write," she explained. "I started remembering street names. The names of people, of pets too. I even remembered the phone number of a person I had spoken to in a dream."

"At first I figured the dreams were from events from my life. Who else would I be dreaming for?" She asked. I shrugged my shoulders and she continued.

"The more information I gathered the more I began to see a pattern. People were making repeat appearances. Houses, events, even motorcycles were the same from one dream to the next. But I didn't know even one person. I was dreaming for somebody else. But who? I had to find out the identity of my dream partner."

Cindy came up with a very creative way to find the answer to her question. "I started taking control of my dreams," she stated. "I would go to sleep with an outline of the dream I wanted to have. A set of questions to be answered." It worked. One night it all came together. I set my mind on getting a hair cut. That way I knew I would see myself in the mirror."

I have to admit it, as much as I was certain she was crazy, she had me hooked. I wanted to learn the identity of her dream partner. I was about to tell her to go on when she continued.

"The person I was dreaming for," she whispered, "is you!"

You could have knocked me over with a feather. I didn't know what to do. Then it came to me. "It was nice talking with you," I stated as I reached for the door handle. I wanted to get as far away from her as possible. "Don't go," Cindy commanded. "I can prove it." I loosened my grip on the handle.

Cindy started telling a story that took place the first Sunday I was in the army. "June 16, 1971. You had KP. It was a hot day and you were on the loading dock when the mess sergeant came to you with a box." I nodded for her to go on. "He asked you if there were any officers around. You didn't know what an officer was. The mess sergeant handed you the box and the keys to his car. 'Put this box in the trunk.' And you did as you were told."

Before I could think of an explanation for her uncanny knowledge of an event that did indeed happen she continued. She told me details from my year in Vietnam to the day at Fort Meade that I got out of the army. "That was Wednesday, 9 June 1971. You had a friend drive you to the bus station. You changed from khaki's to civvies in his car."

"Holy crap," I muttered. Not in disbelief but in belief of something very strange turning out to be true.

Satisfied that I believed her, Cindy leaned against the door. "What do we do now?" she wondered aloud. I doubt she expected an answer from me. If either of us should have an answer it should be her, I reasoned. However, I didn't expect her to have one.

"We're in a rather odd dilemma," I said with a chuckle.

Cindy laughed. "I agree." Then she confessed that she always dreaded this day, the day she came face to face with her dream partner. "I figured out who you were last week. I knew you would be in AMRS today. I thought maybe I wouldn't tell you. Why twist your brain into a pretzel? Then I remember looking at myself in the barbers chair and thinking 'he's not bad looking. And he rides a Harley. So why not let him ask you out and see what happens from there.'"

It was my turn to laugh.

"What's so funny," Cindy asked.

I was quick with my answer. "You'd go out with me?"

"Yes," Cindy shot back.

I chose my next words carefully. "You've lived the last couple of years of my life in your dreams, right?" Cindy nodded in agreement. "Well, this will be the first date I ever went on with the girl already knowing what I want."

The pretty blonde touched my hand. "And this will be the first date you ever went on with the girl already knowing and agreeing to what you want."

The Bet

I got to 'this is the place' a few minutes before six. No sooner had Nancy brought me my first beer than Mike and George walked through the door.

"You're early," Mike greeted me as he took a seat.

George remained standing. He was scoping out the new waitress. "Cute," the recently divorced banker remarked. "Real cute."

"Don't get any ideas," I advised him, "her name is Nancy and she's happily married."

George looked at me as if I had accused him of some hideous crime.

"All I'm saying is she's an attractive young lady."

"We know what you're saying," Mike chimed in. "Now, why don't you take a seat and join us?"

George pulled out a chair and plopped his massive body down in it. "Are you happy?" he asked with a grin.

"So happy," Mike answered, "that I could drink a beer."

"That's just what I'm thinking, that I could drink a beer," George stated loud enough for Nancy to hear him.

The pixy blonde smiled, then turned to the bartender. Moments later she placed beers in front of my two amigos. "Is there anything else you gentlemen would like?" she asked with a smile.

"No thank you," the three of us replied in unison. The three of us watched as Nancy went to another table.

Mike yawned. "I was up to eleven last night grading papers," remarked the high school history teacher. "At the beginning of each year I test the freshmen to find out how much they know about our country's history. Or actually don't know." He paused to take a sip of beer.

"And," I prodded him to continue. He did.

The former paratrooper shook his head. "Sadly, most know very little. One of our future leaders though the US, Germany and Japan had fought against England in our war of Independence."

George chuckled then asked, "You mean they didn't?"

"Screw the war of independence and all wars," I loudly proclaimed, "let's talk bikes."

George and Mike lifted their glasses as did I. "To bikes." Our three glasses clanked.

"The other day I met a guy who just finished riding the iron butt," Mike announced.

"That's a thousand miles in a day?" George asked.

Mike nodded in agreement. "You should have seen the bike the guy was riding. It was some dresser with every creature comfort and electronic device known to man."

"A dresser," I said with mock excitement in my voice. "You mean one of those two wheeled cars with windshield, cruise control, heated grips, radio, CD player and a seat big enough for the circus fat man?"

Mike hoisted his beer. "That's the bike."

"Well I'd like to see him do a thousand miles on a real motorcycle," I quickly added.

Mike put his beer down as George spoke. "A real bike," he repeated. Then he asked, "Like a sportster?" He was looking directly at me.

"What?" I exclaimed. "There's no way on earth that anyone could do a thousand miles in one day on a sportster."

George smiled. "How far do you think you could ride your 1200 in 24 hours?"

I thought for a moment before answering. "Probably five maybe six hundred."

This elicited a laugh from Mike. "There's no way in the world you could ride your little red sportster six hundred miles in one day."

Before I could respond George jumped in. "I'm willing to bet that my, our, good buddy here could ride his little red sportster six hundred miles in one day."

"And how much are you willing to bet?" Mike inquired.

Without hesitation George answered. "A million dollars."

Mike just smiled. "Make that two million and you got yourself a deal." The two men shook hands.

"Excuse me," I said to my softail riding friends. "Who said I will even try riding six hundred miles in one day?"

George and Mike just laughed. "You got to do it," George said, "cause if you do it half my winnings go to you."

"And if you don't do it," quickly added Mike, "half my winnings are your."

I nodded to my drinking companions. "I get a million if I do and a million if I don't. With odds like that I can't lose. Count me in, I'll do it."

My stab at sportster riding immortality began at six the following Saturday morning. George, Mike and I met in the parking lot of a gas station near an on ramp to the interstate.

George kept repeating the obvious, "All you have to do is average twenty five miles per hour."

"I'll be sure to do that when I'm going to the bathroom," I answered as I brought the sportster to life.

Mike looked at his watch then quickly pressed the reset button on the back of the bikes speedometer. "Both A and B are set at zero," he stated.

I shifted into gear. "Ride safe," George called. As I let the clutch out and started across the parking lot I heard Mike holler, "There's no shame in quitting." I had a big smile on my face as I accelerated up the on ramp.

I could not have asked for a better day to ride. Though the morning was cool the day was forecasted to reach a very comfortable seventy. And as a rain storm had gone through two nights earlier there was absolutely no humidity. "Yes indeed," I thought to myself, "this will be a piece of cake."

The first 128 miles were indeed a piece of cake. That's how far I went before stopping for gas. Once back on the road I checked the time. It was eight o one. I quickly did some figuring.

"We're averaging 64 miles per hour," I said aloud. I felt pretty good. As I shifted into fifth my feet went to the highway pegs.

When I stopped for gas 131 miles later my ass was more than a little sore. It was killing me. After filling up the sportster I walked around the convenience store twice. It was all in vain; when I went inside my ass was still sore. "Oh well," I thought to myself, "they don't call it the iron butt for nothing." I bought a bottle of Gatorade which I took outside to drink.

I was about to polish off the Gatorade when a guy riding a dresser pulled up to the pumps. For a couple of seconds I watched as he filled his tank. Then I finished my drink. "Time to go," I said under my breath. I took the key out of my pocket and started for my bike.

"You going on the run?" A voice called across the parking lot.

I turned. The other biker was looking at me. "You going on the run?" He called a second time.

I shook my head in the negative. "No. Just out for a ride."

The guy took the nozzle out of the tank. "It's a great run."

"Thanks for the invite," I called back, "but no can do."

He shrugged his shoulders and I got back on my bike.

The next 117 miles were sheer torture. I rode with my feet on the highway pegs. I rode with my feet hanging straight down and just skimming the blacktop. I even rode bent over the gas tank with my feet on the passenger pegs. It didn't matter, no matter how I sat my ass hurt.

After filling up I walked next door to the local BK. While I ate my whopper I did a little math. I had traveled 376 miles in just under six hours. I was more than pleased with my time. Then I did a little more math. Again I was pleased with the results. The sportster was averaging right at 55 miles per gallon.

I spent more than an hour relaxing in that BK. The whole time I was there I kept drinking water. I must have drunk half a gallon because every ten minutes or so I was in the bathroom. After my last visit to the men's room I picked up my helmet from the table and went outside.

When I got to the sportster I stopped and just looked at it. I took the whole bike in. From its 40 spoke wheels, narrow front end, iconic gas tank, dual exhaust, crinkle black cases and flawlessly applied black cherry pearl paint it was in my humble opinion the best looking motorcycle Harley made. That meant it was the best

looking motorcycle on the road. The only fly in the XL's ointment
was its seat. The seat certainly looked good; however, sitting on it
was another story. It was narrow and thinly padded. I dubbed it my
Achilles Heel.

I turned the key and pressed the start button. The narrow v-twin
immediately began dancing in the frame. I climbed on board and
continued my journey.

The morning ride had been south on the interstate. In the afternoon
I changed directions and rode north. Traffic was lighter and moving
faster. I rode many miles stretched out over the gas tank with my
feet on the passenger pegs. Not only was it more comfortable it also
improved my gas mileage.

On a long ride one has plenty of time to think. I solved math
problems, named the 50 states in alphabetic order and wrote letters
that I would never send. About half an hour into the ride north
I realized something; tomorrow was my birthday! With things at
work being so crazy the past couple of weeks I had forgotten all
about it. I rode much of the rest of the ride thinking what I would
like to do tomorrow. The best idea I came up with was to relax by
the pool. Taking a bike ride wasn't even considered. My ass was
killing me!

When I was about fifty miles from my start point the odometer
turned six hundred. I had slowed down and gotten in the right lane
so I could watch the numbers change. I honked the horn two or three
times then exited the interstate. There were a couple of phone calls
to make.

George answered his cell phone sounding out of breath. "You
might want to sit down for this," I announced.

"I am sitting down," Came the big mans reply.

"We just won a million dollars each!"

George let out a whistle. "What's this we bit?" he asked with a
laugh. Then he quickly added: "Where are you?"

I told him and added that I would be at the gas station where I
had started my ride in less than an hour.

"Meet you there," Mike stated as we hung up. I immediately
dialed George. When he picked up I went right to the heart of the
matter. "When you make out my check my name is spelled with
two L's."

A fellow biker once gave me his ten rules of long distance riding. I can't recall if it was rule number four or rule number five that applied here. Anyway, the rule was the last five miles are the longest. And as I had ten times that distance to travel the final leg of my journey was by far the longest.

Things started to go wrong almost immediately after I got back on the road. For no apparent reason the Jeep in front of me started to slow down. As there was a pick up truck on my left I had no choice but to slow down. When the pick up passed the Jeep I switched lanes and accelerated. As I came along side the door less Jeep I looked over and saw why the driver had slowed down. The pretty young lady was applying her make up! I was about to curse her out when she turned to me and smiled. It's impossible for me to get mad at a good looking blonde in shorts that showed lots of leg. All I could do was shake my head and give a half ass smile. I opened the throttle and got as far away from her as possible.

No sooner had I gotten back in the rhythm of driving on the interstate then the cars in front of me began to slow down. 'It couldn't be,' I reasoned to myself, 'more women drivers putting on make up.' It wasn't-there was an accident. Within minutes traffic was at a virtual stop. And it remained that way for a long time. Standing on my tip toes I could see that the three lanes of traffic were being funneled into one. Suddenly one lane or another would shoot ahead. And just as suddenly it too would stop. For more than an hour I was stuck in the traffic jam.

When I finally passed the accident my sporty and I were about at a boil. I quickly shifted through the gears then rolled the throttle opened. In seconds we were doing seventy. I'm certain that the rushing air felt just as good to the engine as it did to me. The rest of the ride on the interstate was uneventful. I exited it where I had entered it that morning. I caught the light red at the end of the off ramp. As I waited for the light to turn green I lifted up my face shield and laughed out loud. "I've done it!" I had traveled 675 miles in one day and on a sportster. In spite of a very sore ass and aching shoulders I felt good. All that remained for me to do was to ride over the overpass and pull into the gas station.

The sportster and I never made it over the overpass. Not at the same time anyway. When the light turned green I started to make my turn. And that's all I remember. The next thing I know two paramedics are placing me on a stretcher. Mike and George were by my side. As the paramedics rolled me to the waiting ambulance my two friends kept reassuring me that 'you're going to be okay.' Then Mike added: "The police have the driver that rear ended you." I lifted my head off the stretcher and looked around. Next to a cop car were two people. One was a policeman, the other evidently the driver of the vehicle that had hit me. She was a pretty young blonde in shorts that showed lots of leg.

Turn around is fair play

I had to chuckle. Cindy was so exhausted she barely had the energy to walk from our hotel room to the diner next door. Twelve days on the back of a stock 1981 low rider will do that to you; especially if the last day was a twelve hour 638 mile day. Once seated in a booth she leaned back and yawned. "Order me a coffee. Black with two sugars," she instructed me through closed eyes.

My normally talkative wife was quiet while I ate. She didn't even comment on the coffee; a usual talking point. However, halfway through my hamburger she did ask how much further we had to go. Before answering I thought for a moment.

"About as far as we traveled today. Maybe a little more, perhaps a little less," I informed her. Cindy's facial expression quickly changed from serene to something less pleasant. Her only comment was a whispered "damn."

She got more bad news the moment we opened the door to our hotel room. The television was turned to the weather channel which was showing the national weather for tomorrow. Our route home was buried under a sea of green. This time Cindy's 'damn' was not whispered.

"Tell you what," I told her as she brushed her teeth, "why don't we get up real early and head out? The storm is coming from behind us so we might be able to stay ahead of it."

Cindy stopped for a second. Then she nodded in agreement. I set the rooms' alarm clock for four.

Fortunately my mental alarm clock went off early. Otherwise I might not have heard it. The soft purring of an engine idling outside the door, the hurried whispers of men working feverishly, the sound of a motorcycle being rolled up a ramp.

A massive bolt of adrenaline shot through my veins. I was out the door and on them in a flash. I doubt the two men had ever been so surprised in their lives. One second they were tying down my Harley in their trucks' bed the next second they were being tackled by an enraged long haired man; one who was as naked as the day he was born.

One guy jumped out of the truck and ran away. However, his partner didn't have a chance. I grabbed onto with all my might and smacked his head into the trucks' cab until he went limp. It was only then that I realized Cindy was screaming for me to stop. "You're going to kill him!"

I looked at her and smiled. My pretty wife was as naked as me. Then I looked at the man I was holding. His face was a bloody mess. I took a deep breath and relaxed my grip.

"Call the cops," I instructed Cindy. She started for the door when my nemesis spoke.

"Don't call the cops. I'll do anything you want." I pulled him up by the collar. Our faces were inches apart.

"What the fuck!" was all that I could think to say.

It rained the entire way home-all 609 miles. Fortunately Cindy and I weren't exposed to the weather. We rode comfortably in our new truck, the truck our low rider had been strapped into when the day began.

The Hospital

Just past Frog Lake on old highway 31 is a fairly nondescript abandoned building. If one looks hard the faded sign above the door can be read. Mike's v-twin hospital. When you walk through the door years, no decades, disappear. Two large and lumpy sofas are on either side of the room. In front of each is a coffee table, atop which are strewn scores of well read biker magazines. Pick through them. Just don't expect any articles about twin cams or even evo models. The most recent issue you'll find will be dated July 1973; I know-I read them all.

From behind the counter Nancy would greet you by name. She was the live in girlfriend of Brian, the owner and head mechanic of Mike's v-twin hospital. You're probably wondering why Brian would name his business Mike's v-twin hospital. Good question; I truly wish I had the answer for you, but I don't.

Along with her duties behind the counter and answering the phone Nancy was also the entertainment coordinator. That meant she placed the LP's on the record player. She was particularly fond of the Doobie Brothers. Oh, Nancy also scored the drugs. A cousin of hers had connections to some heavy drug pusher. Though I spent many an hour in 'the hospital' as it was commonly called, I never popped a pill or smoked a joint. I saw plenty of other customers take advantage of the drugs but I never even drank one of the beers that were offered to me every time I walked through the door.

Brian was an excellent mechanic. That's why he always had plenty of work. Whenever he wrenched on your bike you knew the job was done right. But as there was only so much a man could do Brian hired a kid to help out. Duane was 22, a year older than me, when he started. At first Brian had him do the simple jobs. Duane would change the oil, replace the chains, and wash the bikes. As time went on Mike would show Duane the tricks of the trade.

Duane was a fast learner. He had a natural ability about all things mechanical. Within a few months he was taking on more involved jobs and doing them spot on. By his first anniversary Duane was wrenching on everything from a sportster with a broken tranny to an electrical problem on a dresser. Once I overheard Brian joke to another customer that he might have to start paying Duane.

It had rained earlier in the morning the Saturday I brought my sportster in for an oil change. As Brian was taking apart a super glides' carb Duane rolled the 900 into his side of the bay. Ten minutes later Duane called to me. "Your chain needs replacing." I told him to replace it. "Put on the best one you got." He did.

"It's the best chain on the market," Duane stated as he rolled the XLH out of the bay. "I'd test ride it, but," he continued as he put out the kick stand, "it's raining." I was quick to say that it was okay. "I'm sure you did a good job."

At first the police thought it was a dumb ass mistake on my part. Then upon closer scrutiny they discovered the real cause of the accident. I had not missed shifted, they concluded. My bike failed because of the chain. The master link had not been put on correctly. It snapped apart the instant I opened the throttle leaving me sitting atop a motionless motorcycle in the fast lane of a rain slicked highway.

I cannot remember who carried me into 'the hospital.' Whoever did placed me on a couch. Then everyone stood around and waited for the ambulance.

Before the police left Duane, Brian, Nancy and two customers were under arrest. All were charged with illegal use of drugs. Duane served ten months in the county lock up. Within days after his release he committed suicide. He never forgave himself for smoking that joint while working on my bike.

Brian and Nancy posted bail then fled the state. It is widely believed that they got new identities and relocated to Ohio. They've never been found. That is why the hospital is an abandoned building.

Some cultures believe that the spirit lives forever in the place where the person died. They are correct. That is why I will spend eternity in the hospital reading well worn motorcycle magazines.

Rainy Day Luck

My first Saturday off in more than a month and it rains. It started a few minutes after nine. I was walking to my bike after having eaten breakfast in the best diner in Jersey when a fat raindrop exploded on my neck. "Damn." I muttered aloud. Looking skywards, a single massive black cloud loomed overhead. For a brief moment I debated whether to don my rain gear. Instantly God gave me the answer to my question. It started drizzling, debate over. I unlocked the tour pack and took out my rain suit and helmet. No sooner had I gotten them on then the heavens opened up. The rain came down in buckets. Cars started pulling off to the side of the road.

Within seconds it was a downpour and there I was sitting on my bike! I couldn't ride in this storm and I couldn't retreat back to the diner. I was stuck right where I sat. Fortunately, with my rain suit on and my helmet visor pulled down I was surprisingly dry. Still, there was not much I could do, except sit, feeling like the proverbial lump on a log, and think. My first thoughts were of the ride I had planned for the day. Cruising up the Palisades Interstate Parkway, then returning south through the Seven Lakes Parkway. It's a scenic and relaxing ride. With each passing minute it looked less likely that I would be making that run. Then my thoughts turned to the present. If only I had asked for a second cup of coffee or talked a minute longer with the cashier I would still be inside the diner. Sitting in a booth looking out and saying how lucky I was not to be out in this rain. However, that was not to be. I wondered how many customers were looking at me and laughing, or thinking I was an idiot. That is if they could see me, the rain was coming down so hard it was difficult to see across the parking lot.

After what seemed an eternity the rain finally began to slacken. A glance at the street was enough to tell me, I wasn't going anywhere soon. The street was ankle deep in fast running water. My mind returned to the last couple of minutes inside the diner. After the matronly waitress brought me my check I got up and walked to the cashier. The cashier sat on a stool reading a paper back novel. She was a pretty girl. Slender with long blonde hair tied in a ponytail. When she sensed me coming she put the book down, stood up and smiled. It was a very warm, welcoming smile. I smiled back at her.

"Was everything okay?" She asked as I handed her the check.

I nodded. "Very good food here."

Again that warm and welcoming smile. "I'm glad." She said looking me straight in the face. She was tall, at most an inch shorter than me and I'm close to six foot tall.

I gave her a ten.

She opened the drawer, counted my change.

"Good book?" I asked.

She turned to the stool where she had placed the book she had been reading. She laughed. "It's a dirty romance novel. Silly and stupid."

I started to say something when she again laughed. "It's not mine." She hurriedly explained. "A customer left it here about an hour ago. I'm expecting her to return for it any minute."

It was my turn to laugh. "It's such a silly and stupid romance novel I only read the first hundred pages."

Once again she flashed that smile of hers. "You honestly don't think I'd read something like that?" She added emphasis to her words by casting a disparaging look at the book.

I read her nametag. "Can I call you Cindy?"

She nodded. "Yes. You can. And what can I call you?" She asked.

Just then the owner of the diner joined us. "Everything okay?" He asked. Before I could answer either Cindy's or his question he continued, this time talking directly to Cindy. Sensing that his arrival was a not too subtle hint for me to leave, I walked out of the diner.

"You idiot." I said aloud as the door closed behind me.

Twenty minutes later I was still calling myself an idiot. Had I stayed at the register a couple of minutes longer, at worse, I would now be enjoying a third or fourth cup of coffee. And with a little luck, had I stayed, I might have gotten to know Cindy better. Maybe even asked her out.

The rain went from a slight drizzle to an occasional sprinkle to nothing. Then suddenly the sun reappeared. I checked the street; it was no longer covered in water. "Guess it's time to go." I said to myself. I let out a deep breath, got off the bike. A minute or two later my rain suit was folded and placed inside the tour pack. Back on the bike I brought the kickstand up, turned the ignition on. Before hitting the starter button I paused for a last look at the diner. The pause turned into a long moment. It ended when I kicked out the kickstand, turned off the ignition.

Cindy was still behind the counter when I walked in. She recognized me with a smile. It was, if possible, even warmer and more welcoming than her previous smiles had been.

"Earlier this morning I left a book here. It's a silly, romance novel that no one claims to read. But, I know everyone does read it." Cindy laughed. I continued. "I don't care about getting the book back. I came here to say my name is Derrick and I would like to ask you out."

That evening Cindy and I went on our first date. It was a bike ride, of course. We rode my Electra Glide Classic north on the Palisades Interstate Parkway and then south on the Seven Lakes Parkway. It was the ride I had planned for that morning. Only it was a lot better at night, especially with a very friendly young lady on the back seat.

Webster Pizza

Webster Pizza is a dump. Even Buddy would admit that and he owns the place. Webster Pizza is cold and drafty in the winter and stifling hot in the summer. Fortunately it has the best pizza west of the Hudson River.

I'm a pizza hound. I can and do eat pizza three or four times a week. Hell, who am I kidding, I eat pizza every day. Sometimes twice a day. I've tried other pizza joints but always come back to Webster Pizza. As I said, they got the best pizza. Period.

I grew up and still live in Webster. After graduating from high school I got a job in the town's garage as a mechanic.

My first pay check went as a down payment on a new Harley. A black cherry pearl sportster 1200 roadster with spoke wheels. It's beautiful and I love it. If you've ever ridden past Webster Pizza you've probably seen my bike there.

Not too many people eat inside Webster Pizza. It just looks dirty. Sometimes I wonder how it passes the Board of Health inspections. Most of it's business is take out or delivery. Every once in awhile a customer will eat their food at one of the half dozen or so tables. But not often.

I'm about the only person who regularly eats there. Other than kids from the local high school I mean. So I was more than a little surprised that Friday night when I walked into the place and saw her sitting at a booth. Even from the back I could tell she was a lady. Her hair was beautiful, long and shinny. A blonde.

I made a concentrated effort not to look at her as I went up to the counter to order. "Two slices and a coke," Buddy called to me from in front of one of the ovens. "Got it," I shot back. As I turned to take a seat she spoke. "You must be quite a regular here." Before I could answer she gave me a smile that could brighten the day of a whore walking the streets of the Vatican.

I can't remember what I said, but I'm sure I muttered something. Again that pretty smile. And a laugh. I was hooked. She gestured that I take a seat. I did.

"I'm on my way home after a long and boring day at work. I still have a twenty minute ride ahead of me." She paused as Buddy brought out our orders. "Lasagna and a diet coke for you and two slices and a coke for you." The pretty lady acknowledged Buddy with a wink and a softly spoken 'thank you.'

When he left she continued. What she said nearly floored me. "I'm looking for some excitement. Now it's either you or the next good looking guy with a stiff dick that walks through that door." Then she casually sipped her soda. "You in or out?"

Though I may have been initially stunned I quickly recovered. I stood up and reached for her hand. "Let's go." She took my hand and followed me out the door.

When she saw my bike she stopped. "I live two minutes from here," I started to explain when she put her fingers to my lips. "Get in," she gestured to her car, a Chevy. I hopped in. She started the engine then turned to me. "I don't have the time to go to your house. Just tell me how to get to a lovers lane or a deserted building." Then she reached over and started rubbing my dick. "We're going to do it in the car."

"Turn right out of the lot," I directed her as my mind frantically raced searching for a spot to park. The abandoned warehouse by the railroad tracks came to mine. "Now make a left." The pretty blonde did as I instructed. "Slow down. When you cross the railroad tracks make a right. The road ends at the river."

I did not learn her name that night. When I asked she said it was not important. What was important, she stated, was that I fuck her hard. I did my best. She seemed satisfied. When she dropped me off next to my bike she asked a funny question. "Can you remember eight fifteen?"

Somewhat puzzled I answered, "sure."

"Good," she responded," that's what time I'll be here next Friday."

I just smiled.

"I take that as a 'yes,'" she grinned.

"Damn right that's a yes," I affirmed.

She shifted the transmission into drive. "Next time I'll be dressed to go on your Harley." She squealed the tires as she drove off.

She was true to her word almost to the second. According to the clock on my speedometer the sexy blonde's Chevy entered the parking lot seconds before the numbers changed to eight fifteen.

Also true to her word she was dressed to take a ride on a motorcycle. In lieu of her skirt and silk blouse that she wore the previous week she was now dressed in jeans and T-shirt." "Will I need my jacket?" she asked the moment she stepped out of her car. "Better bring it. It's always better to have than to want," I advised her.

There's plenty of pretty country around Webster. However, we didn't see much of it. I remember glancing at the clock just as my companion leaned forward. "This has been fun. Now let's fuck." It was eight thirty two.

When we returned to the parking lot, even before I shut down the bike, she again said "eight fifteen." And again I just smiled. A minute latter I was sitting on my sporty watching her tail lights disappear into the night.

"Damn, I'm the luckiest guy in the world," I thought to myself as I pressed the XL's start button.

We met every Friday night at eight fifteen for three or four weeks before I learned her name. Cindy. Over the next couple of weeks we started to talk. Little by little she opened up. She was married, she admitted one night as we waited at a red light. It was something I had suspected all along.

"He's a cop. A state cop," she told me. When the light changed to green she continued. "He's also a thug and a racist." We drove in silence down the county road.

When Cindy slowed down to let a car turn in front of us she turned to me. "You're probably thinking I'm having sex with you to get back at my husband."

"Now that you mention it, yes, that thought has crossed my mind." I stated truthfully.

Cindy flashed her enchanting smile. "You're right."

Ten minutes later all talking stopped, we were having our best sex yet.

Cindy was most definitely married. I met her husband the following Monday evening. Per my normal routine I was in the parking lot of Webster Pizza. I had just shut off my sporty when a commanding voice called my name. I turned and there he was. He was a big man who did not look either happy or friendly.

Our conversation was brief. First he stated the facts. "You've been screwing my wife every Friday night for weeks." Then he stated the threat. "I'm a cop. I found you and I know where you live. If you so much as look at her again I'll kill you." Then he turned, walked back to his car and drove off.

That Friday night at eight fifteen I made certain to be nowhere near Webster Pizza. A friend and I took a bike ride. It was quarter till two Saturday morning when I parked the Harley in the garage. Less than a minute later I was opening an envelope that had been placed in my door handle.

"Where were you? You better be there next Friday at eight fifteen." Though the note was not signed I knew who had written it.

I didn't get much sleep that night. If I see her again that goon of hers' will kill me. And if I don't see her, there's no telling what she'll do. Either way, I figured, I was screwed.

That next week was hell. I was in a mess and I knew it. An old saying kept racing through my mind. Be careful what you wish for. It may come true. I, like every other guy I suspect, had always dreamed of meeting a beautiful woman. And screwing her brains out. Meeting Cindy was a dream come true. She was beautiful and she loved to fuck. Only one problem, there was a fly in the ointment. The beautiful woman who loved to fuck had a husband!

When Friday rolled around I knew what I had to do. I would tell Cindy that I had the pleasure of meeting her husband and that after a brief but frank discussion we had reached a consensus. I would not see her again. Ever. I figured whatever she could do was not half as bad as what her husband would do.

I was parked in my usual spot in front of Webster pizza at seven fifty seven. And there I sat for the next two hours, waiting for a blonde who never came. At ten o'clock I called it quits. I entered

Webster, ate a slice and then jumped on my bike. I cannot remember a more relaxing ride than the one I took that night. It felt like a heavy load had been taken off my shoulders.

I didn't get home till a few minutes after two. And when I got home there were three state police cars parked in front of my house. My serenity was instantly shattered.

I had barely stopped my bike when I was surrounded by a sea of blue clad men. Their leader, a tall lieutenant who looked like he could play fullback for the Giants, wasted no time.

His first question was if I knew Cindy Mangullis. I was truthful. "I know a Cindy but I don't know her last name."

The LT snorted. "You've been fucking a woman for four months and you don't know her last name." A red haired sergeant laughed.

"That's right," I stated. More chuckles from the peanut gallery.

The LT was quick to change tracks. "Do you own a 38 caliber pistol?"

I shook my head. "No. I don't own any guns. Now will you tell me what this is about?"

The lieutenant continued. "This woman you've been screwing for the past four months but don't know her last name, well she turned up dead tonight. And since you were screwing her every Friday night and tonight is Friday we figured we'd stop by your place and have a little chat with you."

"Holy fuck," was all I could mutter. Then I told the lieutenant everything I knew. Told him every detail of tonight's ride. No detail was too small for me to omit. I was quick to pull out the gas receipt from when I filled the Harley. "The time stamp is eleven twelve," I pointed out. The LT took the piece of paper from my hand. As he studied it I continued. I named the waitress who waited on me at the diner where I ate a burger. "It cost seven something. I gave the waitress a ten and told her to keep the change." I must have convinced the cops because when they left I was still home. When the last cop car turned the corner I started the sportster. There was no way in the world I was going to sleep after this much excitement. I rode till the sun crested the horizon.

Cindy's murder and the arrest of her husband were the headlines for the Sunday papers. She was described as a former cheerleader who after graduating from college worked as an insurance adjuster. She was just 26 years old, two years older than me. Her alleged murderer was described as a nine year veteran of the state police and a semi pro boxer. They had been married three years.

I've just been notified that I will be called to testify at the trial. It's not something that I am eager to do. However, if it will help bring a killer to justice I will do it.

Sitting at my usual table in Webster Pizza, as I am now, I can not help but think of Cindy. Though our relationship was primary just sex I do have a very nice memory of her. It was a stormy Friday night and she was driving us to our favorite fuck spot. Spotting an elderly gentleman walking on the shoulder of the highway she stopped. 'Hop in,' she told the guy. The soaked guy got in the back seat. Cindy turned the heat up full blast as she drove him to his apartment which was about a mile away. The guy was very appreciative. "It's coming down in buckets," he informed us. I was very surprised by Cindy's kind act and told I her so. Her answer was short but sweet. "It seemed like the right thing to do," was all she said.

I have also learned something from this tragedy. From now on I'll be a bit more leery of beautiful women who just want to screw. Yeah, like that will ever happen again. Hold it a second. A former cheerleader I went to high school with just walked through the door. Though I cannot remember her name I certainly remember her in her skimpy cheerleader uniform. She looked good then and she looks good now. "Is that your Harley Mitch?" she is quick to ask. Before I can answer she continues. "I bet it would be so much fun to go for a ride around the reservoir."

Harley Riding Sheriff

I was born and raised in Webster. Other than the three years I served in the army I've lived my entire life here. Webster is a good town to live in. There are tree lined streets, well maintained homes, a nice park and good people. A lot of good people.

Webster has a population of about six thousand. I know many by name and most by sight. That's one of the advantages of being the town's sheriff.

I became a deputy after I returned from Desert Storm. Mike Roman was the sheriff and Jeff Turner was the other deputy back then. Two years after pinning on my badge Jeff went into the state police and Mike retired. At 23 I became the sheriff of Webster.

Other than speeders on the highway that runs through Webster my work days are pretty routine. An occasional illegally parked car or truck, a lost dog, stuff like that. In the nearly twenty years I've been in law enforcement I can count the number of serious crimes on the fingers of my hands. And have fingers left.

That's not to say we don't have crime. Webster is not immune to what goes on in the rest of the country. Fortunately, must of the crime is petty. A kid caught smoking dope, a teenage girl getting back at her parents by knocking over a dozen mail boxes, a group of young adults breaking into the pizza shop.

Webster's most serious crime was a fight between two men that nearly turned deadly. Both men had been drinking heavy and both were involved with the same woman. Things had been brewing for days between the two men before it finally exploded on a Friday night.

One man sliced the other man with a knife. The bleeding man responded by pulling out a pistol. He fired six times at point blank range and managed to hit the man once and that was a glancing shot. Then the two men went at it with their fists.

When my deputies and I arrived the living room looked like it had been hit by a bomb. It was destroyed. And the two combatants were no better. Both were black and blue and bleeding, but they would live.

That was the most serious crime I can remember. That is until last summer. A couple walking along the river found a body. The body turned out to be George Miller.

George was in his early thirties. He owned and operated a small motorcycle repair shop at the edge of town. He worked exclusively on Harley's and most of his customers belonged to clubs. Outlaw clubs.

I had been in his shop many times and not always on business. Like George and his customers I too rode a Harley. What brought me to his shop was his work and prices. George was a good mechanic and his price was far better than the authorized dealer.

Whenever I walked through the front door someone would call out 'quick hide the dope the cops are here!' Everyone would laugh, including me. I never had trouble with George or any of his customers. Whenever they would spot me riding my sportster they would wave.

The only time I had a law enforcement reason for entering his shop was when someone spray painted his walls with graffiti. When George and I viewed the walls we both chuckled. "I think," George said, "that our criminal is an idiot." Whoever had done the crime had written 'screw Harely-Davidsen,' and 'have sex with yurself.'

My two deputies, John Hansen and Cindy Coats, and I devoted ourselves to solving George's murder. We were assisted by the state police and the FBI's anti-gang unit. The FBI was under the belief that because George rode a Harley and worked on outlaws bikes he was murdered by an outlaw. Their lead investigator told me he believed that George must have screwed over a club member.

"I think you're wrong," I told the FBI agent. "George was as straight as an arrow. He never caused any problems with me or with any of his customers. How do I know this? I know this because I've been one of his customers for years. And I know many of his customers by name."

The agent shrugged off my comments. However, six months later he was called back to headquarters. A few weeks late the state police closed their investigation. The morning after they left I called John and Cindy into my office. "If this crime is ever going to be solved we're going to be the ones to do it. Always remember, George was murdered in our town." Webster's police force was not going to let his killer go unpunished.

Though I knew from the start that George's customers hadn't committed the crime and that the FBI agent had interviewed scores of bikers I went back to them. I talked with them at the shop, which was being run by his brother Jim, in bars, at their homes. Where ever and whenever was convenient for them I was there.

I interviewed bikers at their homes, at gas stations and one happy biker who was getting a lap dance from a six foot tall blonde. More than a few interviews started with the biker stating 'I told that FBI agent everything I know.' I would spend the next five minutes explaining why I was talking with him again.

"I know you and the other bikers didn't do it. I'm doing this because his killer is still out there and I want him caught. And as a fellow biker I would think you'd want this piece of crap in jail."

Fortunately my prior good relations with the bikers paid off. I got several pieces of information that the FBI agent missed. I followed every lead. All dead ended.

A year has passed since George Miller had his throat slit. No one has been held accountable for his murder. The state police and FBI have long since given up on solving the crime. Even the Webster Sheriff's Office has put it on the back burner. It appears that our only chance of putting the murderer away is if he walks into our office and confesses.

Funny thing, he has walked in our office and now he's confessing to you.

The Ride to the Big Ditch

Mike was always right on time. Late. This morning was no exception. He was supposed to be at my apartment at eight. "You sure you can make it that early?" I had asked him when we spoke on the phone yesterday afternoon. "I don't want you to miss your beauty sleep." I heard my erstwhile friend laugh through the receiver. "Don't worry. I'll see you tomorrow morning at eight sharp." He assured me. We hung up.

At eight sharp I was standing next to my low rider in front of my garage. The minutes ticked by and Mike was nowhere to be seen. Or heard. He was always heard before he was seen. My long time riding partner runs after market pipes on his 'glide. I went inside the apartment to take a leak, glanced at the kitchen clock. 8:17. "Earth to Mike It's eight twenty. Where are you?" I commented as I went into the bathroom.

I walked back to my bike, sat on the seat. A couple of nights ago I had spent a good two hours cleaning and polishing it. It's chrome and bloodstone red paint shinned in the morning sun. "You're one good looking scooter." I remarked to myself. Mike was always after me about getting a 'modern bike.' My 1981 low rider may not be a modern bike; however, it is a good bike. My dad, the original owner, gave it to me when I graduated from high school. I have no intentions of getting rid of it. It has always gotten me to and from wherever I've asked it to take me. Whereas I've kept my first Harley these past ten years Mike on the other hand buys a new scooter every couple of years. Back in '96 he started out on a very used sportster. He didn't have much luck with that 883. It was one problem after another. Mike was always fixing or replacing something on it. Less than a year later he bought a new 1200. The black sporty was a sharp looking bike; however, Mike didn't keep it long. He stated that he wanted a big twin. Within six months he was on an evo powered super glide. Mike kept that FXR for two or three years then bought a new softail. He rode that bike till April or May of last year when he traded it in on a new twin cam 88 FXD. That's his present ride.

I inserted the key in the ignition. The first thing Mike inevitably calls out when he shows up is, 'let's ride!" It wasn't like we had to be somewhere at a certain time. Today is Sunday. We're just getting together for a ride, like we've done a hundred times before. Maybe we'll ride east, or perhaps we'll head south, or even west. Or than again we could always go north. Living in Flagstaff has its' advantages, you could set off in any direction and have a great ride. My favorite ride is to what Mike calls 'the big ditch.' The big ditch being the Grand Canyon. Not the nearby South Rim, rather the North Rim. It is a four hundred plus mile ride there and back. And what a ride it is. You travel on a serpentine highway through spectacular countryside. At your destination you have the always awe-inspiring beauty of the canyon to look at. Standing on the edge looking out over the incredible work of Mother Nature one feels very small and quite insignificant.

As usual Mike revved his twin cam when he was a block away. It was his way of saying, 'start your engine.' I turned the petcocks handle, put out the kicker arm. The first start of the day is always via the kicker. It's a habit of mine. Two kicks with the ignition off then turn the key to the on position and kick. One kick, that's all it ever takes. This morning was no exception. The eighty-inch shovelhead rumbled to life. Even with its stock pipes it sounded good.

Mike pulled into the driveway and instead of shouting, 'let's ride,' he shut off his bike. "What gives?" I asked above my idling motor. Mike was smiling from ear to ear. "You're probably wondering why I'm late." He began. "Because you're you." I replied with more than a trace of sarcasm in my voice. My dig went in one ear and out the other. "I won't bore you with the details, so here goes. You and I will be taking two young ladies to the big ditch today."

Bore me with the details." I stated as I turned off the engine.

My good friend put the super glide's kickstand down. "You're going to love this."

When he finished I could only smile. Something like what he just described could only happen to Mike. Not wanting to be late this morning Mike went out for gas after talking with me yesterday. When he goes to pay 'a good-looking blonde with an incredible body' gets in line behind him. "I figured I'd be gentlemanly like and say something witty to her. So I turn and blurt out 'it's a cold day.'"

Both Mike and I burst out laughing.

"That's the witty thing you came up with?" I asked in disbelief.

Mike just shrugged his shoulders.

"It's a cold day." I repeated. "On a day that the devil himself would turn the ac on you say 'it's a cold day.'"

"The blonde liked it. She laughed. Then she says 'I know you. You're Mike.'"

"You sure she said that? And not, 'you're an idiot and stop bothering me.'"

Mike ignored my comment, rubbed his nose. "She's the little sister of that accountant I dated last year. Karen. You met her the day we rode to the Hoover Dam."

I drew a blank. Mike continued. "You know, she wore boots and thought we were nuts for wearing sneakers."

Not wanting to belabor the point I signaled for Mike to get on with the story.

He took the hint. "Little sister and I spend a few minutes taking, then I ask if she'd like to get a drink. She couldn't, her girlfriend was at her apartment waiting for her to return. They had to work the afternoon shift at the hospital. They're nurses. Then I ask Miss Incredible Body if she and her girlfriend would like to go for a bike ride tomorrow morning. I even suggested the big ditch." Mike paused dramatically, expecting me to beg him to go on. I remained mute.

"It took a lot fast talking to get her to say yes." My friend blurted out. "They're nurses." He explained. "And you know how nurses hate motorcycles."

"When and where do we meet them," I asked very nonchalantly.

We met Barbara, AKA little sister/Miss Incredible Body and her friend Nancy twenty minutes later at their apartment. Nancy opened the door with a cup of coffee in her hand. A moment later Barbara joined her. Introductions were made. Both girls were very attractive. They were tanned and appeared quite fit. However, I'd give the edge to Barbara. There's something about a blonde that does it for me. Nancy put her coffee cup down. "I'm ready." She turned to Barbara. "Are you ready?" The smiling blonde nodded. We left the apartment.

As we walked to the bikes Barbara commented that they were 'pretty.' Mike and I grinned. Then Barbara quickly added. "Especially the red one." The grin instantly vanished from Mike's face. Mike's FXD is jet black.

"That's my bike." I stated.

Barbara looked at both bikes then at Nancy.

"Whatever bike you choose is fine with me." Nancy said.

Barbara didn't hesitate. "I want to ride on this bike." She pointed to my low rider.

Mike shrugged his shoulders, smiled at Nancy. "Hop on." He told his date who quickly threw a leg over the super glide's seat.

Barbara climbed onto the shovelhead. "Let's ride." Mike called to me. The two bikes fired as one.

Mike and I have been riding together for a good many years. We know each other's moves by heart. Usually he'll ride up front which is fine with me. Today he let me lead the way. Traffic was light and we settled in for a relaxing ride on highway 89. No sooner had I put my feet to the highway pegs than Barbara leaned over my shoulder.

"We got a great day for riding." She stated. I couldn't have agreed more.

I nodded in the affirmative. "Everyday is great for riding."

"I've lived in Mesa all my life, well, except for going to college, and I've never been to the Grand Canyon. I'm pretty excited about going. I'm also pretty excited about riding on a motorcycle. I've never been on one before."

I was about to answer when suddenly a car pulled out of a gas station right in front of me. I had to use both brakes and dump two gears to avoid hitting the Nissan. Mike slingshot passed me, then fell in along side me. "Idiot!" He shouted as the Nissan driver accelerated. The guy in the car flipped us the bird. Mike returned the gesture. Knowing my buddy, his blood was boiling. If Mike were riding solo he'd catch up to that guy and discuss safe driving with him in a most energetic way. However, with Nancy on the back seat he wasn't about to jeopardize her safety. Instead he turned to me. "That guy couldn't have waited ten seconds for us to pass." He remarked shaking his head.

"I don't know what he was thinking." I called back over the rumble of my exhaust pipes.

A minute later Mike dropped back and we continued our ride north.

Barbara leaned forward. "You're a good driver." She said.

I turned to her and smiled. "Thank you. Years of experience. Much of it learned the hard way." I confessed.

Barbara returned my smile, then she began to rub my shoulders. "Feels good?" She asked.

"Yes!" I moaned in fake ecstasy.

Much to my delight Barbara continued rubbing my shoulders. She was doing so when Mike pulled up along side me. Turning in his direction he signaled for us to pull over. I put my right directional on and turned into the parking lot of an abandoned convenience store. Mike stopped his super glide along side me. Neither Mike nor I shut off our bikes.

"Didn't we just miss the road to the Grand Canyon?" Nancy called.

"That's the road to the south rim." I informed her. "We're going to the north rim."

Nancy thought over what I had just said. "You mean there are two rims?"

There was a moment of silence. Then the four of us busted out laughing.

"Did I really just say what I think I said?" Nancy said sheepishly.

The remainder of the ride passed uneventful, save for watching the beauty of the Vermillion Cliffs National Monument unfold before us.

"Very pretty," Barbara commented as she pointed to the distant cliffs.

At two that afternoon the four of us were gazing into the abyss that is the Grand Canyon. Neither Barbara nor Nancy had ever been there before. Both were duly impressed. "It's incredible." Barbara stated as we looked out over the edge. "Truly incredible." Then she turned to me and quickly added, "So was the ride."

For reasons I'll never understand the ride south to Flagstaff went quicker than the ride north to the Grand Canyon. And that included stopping for a late lunch. When we reached their apartment Karen and Barbara gave us the proverbial bum's rush. One minute the two girls were standing alongside us the next minute Mike and I were watching as they closed the door behind them. "Not even a look back." Mike commented rather dejectedly. I agreed. "Well let's ride over to Smitty's for a glass or two of sorrow beer." I suggested as we fired our bikes. Mike was always up for a beer. Or two.

Half an hour later we were on our second beers when BH walked in. I quickly called him to our table. BH was a good guy who occasionally rode with us. However, that wasn't the reason I wanted to speak with him tonight. BH was an orderly who worked in the same hospital as Barbara and Karen. Maybe he knew them and could shed some light on their behavior.

"Sure I know Barbara and Karen." BH said with a smile. "Everyone knows them."

Mike put his beer down. "Well for creeps sakes tell us what you know."

"They're pretty hot, aren't they? Tall, healthy and friendly." BH continued, much to the dismay of Mike and me.

"BH, out with it." I interjected.

Our friend leaned across the table, picked up Mike's glass, took a long chug from it. Then he drank from my glass. After licking his lips he suggested we take a good drink too. Mike and I hesitated.

"No, go on." He urged. "You'll need it." Mike and I obliged.

"I hate to tell you this but Barbara and Karen are hot all right," BH paused for dramatic effect, "but for each other."

Mike and I were speechless. BH broke the silence. "Sorry to break the news to you but it's the truth. Every guy in the hospital has tried to pick up on them." Then he reached across the table for Mike's beer. Mike's grabbed the glass first, hoisted it to his mouth.

"You're right," he said to BH, "I do need it." When he empty glass he slammed it to the table.

"Well I'll be a monkey's uncle." Mike stated with a laugh.

"Listen," I said slowly, "we had a great ride. So what if our dates were not our dates?

All is not lost. There's plenty of beer and the night is young."

A True Friend

Today was a beautiful summer's day in the northeast. The temperature was in the mid to upper seventies, the sky was clear and there was the gentlest of breezes. Best of all there was a total absence of humidity! It was a day meant to ride and I intended to do just that.

Around noon three of my buddies were coming over on their rice rockets. They had planned a day of screaming down twisty roads at the end of which we'd stop and have more than a couple of beers. Last year I lived for such days. My life revolved around working, going to college and riding my 750 on the weekends. Riding my bike meant pushing it and me to the max, and then some. More than a few times my guardian angel came to my rescue when I pushed too hard.

That was last year, a lifetime ago. A lot has happened in the past twelve months. For one, my guard unit was mobilized and sent to Iraq. While processing at Fort Dix my folks sold my Honda for me. I figured I wouldn't need it where I was going. With the money from the sale, plus what I would save in the desert my next bike would be a screamer. And there would be a next bike-only thing-I didn't know what it would be.

Our set up in Iraq wasn't bad. Being in a medical unit has its' advantages. The top two were decent food and air conditioning. Everyone did his or her job and the time passed quickly and very fortunately without mishap. I became pretty tight with sergeant James, one of the mechanics in the motor pool. Sergeant James rode a Harley electra glide. "A land yacht," I called it. James just laughed.

Then he told me all the places he had ridden to and the trip he was planning once he got home. James got a lot of mail. Members of his HOG chapter wrote him regularly. They also sent him plenty of care packages. Among the goodies included were Harley oriented magazines and brochures. Whenever James got a package he would invite me to stop by after work to check out the motorcycle related materials.

At first I found it less than interesting to read about Harley's. The thought of sitting on a couch glide doing the speed limit didn't appeal to me. Still, I'd thumb through the magazines and talk bikes with James. It was a good way to pass the time-talking bikes that is. Every once in awhile James would show me a picture of a Harley he thought was good looking. I'd check it out and then ask how fast could it go. One night about half way through our tour James listened to me ask that question one time too many. He put his magazine down and turned to me. "Listen, when are you going to start enjoying life instead of speeding through it? If all you want to do is to go fast, buy a Yamaha or Honda. However, if you ever get to the point where you want to enjoy the ride, the scenery and the other riders, a Harley is the way to go."

To be honest, at first, I just blew off the good sergeant's words. Then I started to think them over. A couple of days later I had to admit, he had hit the nail on the head. All the rides I had taken were the same. From start to finish they were endless bursts of speed and massive adrenaline rushes. I cannot recall ever getting on my bike just to enjoy the ride, or to check out the scenery. And the friends I rode with? They were either trying to pass me or I was attempting to pass them.

The next time James and I got together I picked up the Harley brochure. Then I asked him a question I am certain he never expected to hear. "Okay, Mr. Harley, tell me what is the best bike for a 22 year old who wants to go fast and yet enjoy the ride?" We talked long into the night and the next night as well. We discussed Buell's, but quickly discounted them. "Too much like a rice rocket." The same went for the V-Rod's. Electra glides weren't even mentioned. Then James gave me the history as well as the pros and cons of the sportster. Then he did the same for the super glides and softails. When all was said and done I had decided on the sportster 1200 roadster.

That was the bike I was going to ride this morning when there was a knock on the front door. My mother answered it. "It's Barbara." My mother called to me. Barbara is our neighbor. She's 14 or 15, I can't recall. I remember she just had a birthday, something she had written about in one of the letters she sent me. She wrote me pretty often when I was overseas. She even sent me five or six care packages. All in all Barbara is a good kid. We talked for a few minutes in the living room then I asked if she would like to see my bike. She eagerly said she would love to see it.

When I opened the garage door Barbara let out a whistle. "It's very pretty." She commented. I couldn't agree more. Then I gave her the fifty-cent tour of the bike along with a brief history of the sportster. When I finished Barbara was impressed. "You sure know a lot about motorcycles." I smiled and silently thanked sergeant James.

"I was just about to clean it. A bunch of us are going for a ride this afternoon." I explained as I picked up the bottle of wax.

"Would you like me to help?" She asked.

I nodded. "Sure. Grab the bottle of chrome cleaner and jump right in."

The bike had less than 50 miles on it. Not only was the bike brand new it was immaculate. I had picked it up from the dealer last night and as it was expected to rain I rode it straight home. No sooner had I parked it in the garage then the heavens opened up. Man, it came down in buckets! Still Barbara and I cleaned and waxed it. My young friend even cleaned the spokes!

Barbara and I did more than just clean a motorcycle. We talked. Barbara told me about the things that were new and exciting in her life. Hearing her speak brought a smile to my face. It was like reading one of her letters. What was most surprising to me was the fact that I actually knew quite a bit about her. And what I knew, I liked. She was good to her friends and parents alike. She was also very good to me. Barbara had made time every four or five days to write me a letter. I am not talking about e-mail or writing a letter on the computer and having it printed out. When Barbara wrote a letter she did so with pen in hand. She also put together the packages she sent me. The contents of which were paid for with her money she earned babysitting.

During a lull in the conversation I thought back to something sergeant James had stated one night so long ago.

"Barbara, if your parents say it's okay I'd like to take you for a ride. Would you like to go?"

The young lady didn't know what to say. Then she put down the towel she was using. "I'll be right back." She quickly started towards her house.

"Hang on a second." I called after her. "I want to hear that it's okay from their lips."

Barbara's parents were cool with their daughter going for a 'short' ride. "Just be careful." They stated.

As we started across Barbara's lawn two rice rockets pulled into my driveway. Mike and George had arrived. Mike lifted his visor. "Andy couldn't make it. He's helping his father around the yard."

Before introductions could be made George started in.

"How are you going to keep up with us?" He asked as he looked over my XL.

Mike was even more blunt. "My lord, a Harley slowster." He remarked as he surveyed my 1200.

I let their remarks go in one ear and out the other. "Mike, George this is Barbara. She's going with me." I went into the garage and got two helmets. As I handed one to Barbara George pulled me to the side. He wanted to know if I was serious about taking Barbara. "Yes." I answered. "She's just a kid." He stated. I glanced at Barbara. She looked like she was expecting something bad to happen. She knew the conversation was about her.

I told George that Barbara was more than just a kid. "She's a good friend." I explained but to no avail. George just didn't get it. He couldn't get past her age.

"Gary, maybe I shouldn't go." Barbara interjected.

I turned to my neighbor. Moments ago she had been very excited about her first motorcycle ride. Now, despite her smile, I knew she was expecting me to tell her 'some other time,' or 'later.' What chance was there that I would take her riding rather than ride with my two friends?

I knew what I was had to say. It would be difficult, however, I also knew it was the right thing to say. So I just said it.

"Listen guys, Barbara is coming with me-with or without you."

A minute later the two brightly colored land rockets accelerated down the street. With them went two so-called friends. However, in reality George and Mike and Andy weren't my friends. If they were they would have written me once or twice when I was overseas. And Andy would have stopped by to say 'welcome home.' No, George, Mike and Andy weren't friends, they were just guys I raced with.

About half an hour later Barbara and I stopped at a Dairy Queen. I bought my 15-year-old friend the biggest banana split ever made. She laughed as I kept telling the girl making it to put more whipped cream on it. As we sat down to eat our ice cream Barbara thanked me for taking her.

"No, thank you." I told her.

She didn't understand so I recounted the night sergeant James had his little talk with me. "The good sergeant said when I was ready to enjoy the ride, the scenery and the other riders I would be ready for a Harley. Well, I'm enjoying the ride. And the scenery is pretty. But most of all I'm enjoying the person I'm riding with."

Lucky Day

Last night it rained and the wind blew like the devil himself was coming to end the world. This morning dawned calm, sunny and bright. It was as if God himself had a picnic planned for the day. I took the blue skies and cool temperature as a harbinger of a great day. It certainly had the beginnings of one. Though at first things were a little strange in the end it turned out that my instinct was correct. It was a great day.

It was a few minutes before eleven when I kicked started my low rider to life. The stock 80 inch shovelhead sounded good. "A little mute, but good." I mumbled under my breath as I folder the kicker arm out of the way. Seconds later I brought the clutch lever in, tapped the gear shifter and slowly opened the throttle. My days ride to nowhere in particular had begun.

It's kind of funny that my bloodstone red FXS will take me anywhere I want to go. That is as long as there is gas in it's tanks. No sooner had I turned the corner than the low rider spat and coughed. Instinctively I dropped my left hand to the petcock and turned the lever to reserve. That quickly remedied the situation. When I came to 5ᵗʰ Street I went straight instead of turning right. The interstate would have to wait. Stan's gas station was just up the block.

When I stopped at the pump an attractive blonde walking on the sidewalk caught my eye. Dressed in halter top and skin tight jeans the young lady was definitely a head turner. "Wow. You are one fine looking woman." I stated aloud. "I certainly would like to get to know you." There is an old adage; beware what you wish for-you may get it. In retrospect I should have adhered to that saying. However, I didn't.

The blonde turned in my direction. A smile came over her pretty face. Then she waved and called what I thought could have been my name. She started walking towards me. I put down the kickstand and smiled.

Now it's not often that I'm speechless. Usually I can shoot the bull with the best of them. However, this morning at Stan's gas station I was speechless. For a good five minutes I stood in silence as the shapely young lady carried on a one way conversation with herself. My mind raced on three levels. I tried to listen to her, tried to figure out who she was and last but not least tried to figure out a way to get her on the back of my bike.

Nothing she said gave me any clues to her identity. One moment she was talking about a brother in Tucson; the next thing I knew she was telling how much she hated school. Then she went on about a girl friend that just broke up with her boyfriend. Even with the hundred bits of information she put out I still could not place her.

When she paused to rub her nose I blurted out the $64,000 question. "I'm sorry, but who are you?"

Now it was the young lady's turn to be speechless. "I'm Cindy. Cindy Jenkins." she said emphatically.

My mind raced even faster than before. It searched every nook and cranny of my gray matter. All in vain. No where in my life did I know or hear of a Cindy Jenkins. I didn't have to verbalize my answer. The blank look on my face was easy enough to read and Cindy read it correctly.

There was an awkward moment of silence. Cindy broke it when she asked who I was.

I told her. It took Cindy only a second to process my answer. She smiled, then chuckled. Then she started laughing. She laughed so hard that tears streamed down her cheeks and still she laughed. When she finally regained her composure she simply said, "I thought you were my sister's old boyfriend. Sorry." She smiled then turned and resumed walking down the sidewalk.

My eyes would have continued following her had not the guy in the Chevy behind me honked his horn. "Are you going to fill your bike or not? He called. "Screw it," I muttered under my breath. In a flash I duck walked the Harley past the pump, put down the kick stand and got off the bike. "There, you can fill up now," I shouted to the guy in the Chevy. Then I turned my attention to the pretty blonde. "Cindy! Wait!" I called.

She waited.

Cindy and I talked a few minutes before she was throwing one of her long legs over the Harley's seat. I pressed the electric start and off we went. Everything was coming together, the makings of a perfect ride. The Fat Bob's were full, the shovelhead was purring, the Arizona scenery was beautiful and holding on tight to me was a blonde who was giving all the right signals.

However, the promised good time was not to be. At least not with Cindy. And in retrospect I can only say 'thank God.'

I had just passed an 18 wheeler when Cindy leaned forward. "I'm hungry." She spoke into my ear. I nodded then took the next exit off the interstate. At the bottom of the off ramp was a McDonalds.

Cindy was sipping on her shake when she made a comment that put an abrupt and complete end to my plans for a fun filled afternoon. "Next Thursday is my birthday." She said. Before I could say 'congratulations' she continued: "I'll be fifteen." She smiled; I nearly crapped my pants.

We finished our meal in record time. Then at speeds well above the posted limit I returned Cindy to the spot where we had met. The very cute and very under aged blonde climbed off the bike. Seconds after she thanked me for 'the neat ride and lunch' she left. I watched as she resumed her walk towards I know not where-a walk I should never have interrupted.

When Cindy turned a corner and disappeared from sight I let out a sigh of relief. I quickly got my thoughts together. It didn't take me long to realize where I needed to be and what I needed. I needed to be at 'Frogs Place' having a beer.

The second I walked through the front door Linda greeted me with a smile. "You look like you could use a cold one." She called. I nodded in agreement as I took a seat at the bar.

"Linda," I began after I took a sip of beer, "you're a mind reader." The barmaid laughed.

"You think I don't know the one thing a biker wants when he walks through the front door?" She asked with a grin.

It was my turn to laugh. I tapped the glass of beer with my fingertip. "You're partially right." I slowly took another sip of beer. "But there are two things a biker wants when he walks through the front door." When I continued there were grins on both our faces. "Especially if you're behind the bar."

I'm going to end my story here. You'll have to figure out for yourself what happened next. And I'm certainly not going to tell you what went on later that night. Suffice it to say that the second half of my day was a lot better than the first half. However, I will tell you one thing. Linda was glad that this biker walked through the front door.

Serendipity

S erendipity is a word that just sounds nice. And it has a nice meaning to it. According to Mr. Webster serendipity means 'finding something good accidentally.' Not too long ago I had a serendipity moment. And it happened in perhaps the most unlikely of places.

In early July my parents moved into an assisted living facility. At first they were more than a little upset about leaving the home they had lived in for more than sixty years. However, they quickly made friends and adjusted to their new surroundings.

My wife and I visit them nearly every day. Barbara is a nurse who works in the hospital directly across the highway from the facility. She helps with their medical care. Barbara also rides a Harley as do I.

A few weeks after mom and dad moved into the facility Barbara and I knew many of the other residents by name. Often we would spend a few minutes talking with them as we made our way to my parent's apartment. As I am a history buff and many of the elderly men are veterans I would ask about their time in the service.

I would also joke with them. If the day was hot and the sky cloudless I'd ask if they were ready for the snow storm. Or if the day was cool and cloudy I'd ask if they were going swimming.

This past Saturday morning Barbara and I rode our bikes to visit mom and dad. As we walked through the hallway an elderly gentleman opened his door. Barbara stopped and greeted him with a warm, "Good morning." The man appeared pleasantly surprised.

"Good morning to you," he replied as he righted his walker. Barbara and I started to leave when he gestured to our helmets.

"Do you have a motorcycle?" He asked.

The two of us turned. "We both do," answered Barbara.

Her answer brought a smile to the elderly mans' face.

"Do you have a motorcycle?" I asked him with a grin.

The senior citizen smiled. "Not anymore. Had to sell it."

Both Barbara and I were intrigued. "What did you have?"

"Harley-Davidsons!" he shot back without hesitation. Then he posed the ten thousand dollar question. "What else is there?"

Barbara and I did visit my parents that morning. About ten minutes later then we had planned. That was about how long we spent talking with Walter about his life, his wife and of course his Harley's.

After Walter he got out of the army he bought a knucklehead. He rode it from Fort Knox, Kentucky to Albany, New York. "That's where I was from," he explained. Walter went to college and became a teacher, a teacher who in 1957 bought one of the first sportsters.

Over the years Walter continued to ride. "I was single and liked to travel. Fortunately I had the time and the money to do it." He then recited the states and places he had ridden to. Barbara and I were in awe.

"When I got married," he told us with a far away look in his blue eyes, "my wife and I rode to Atlantic City for our honeymoon. She was a beautiful woman who fortunately loved to ride." I turned to Barbara and smiled.

Walter's last bike was a 1994 low rider. "A few weeks after I got it I rode it to see my brother in Florida. He lives just outside of Daytona. From there I went to Kansas to visit with an old army buddy. Then I rode it back to Albany." I was impressed.

"That was quite a ride," Barbara acknowledged.

Walter looked at my wife. "It was a lot of fun. After coming home I knew it was time to put the bike away. I was 70 and the Harley was too heavy for me to hold up."

I glanced at my watch. "It was certainly nice meeting and talking with you, but we have to go. My parents are expecting us." We shook hands and parted.

Later that morning as Barbara and I left through the buildings front door a voice called to us. It was Walter. He was sitting in one of the chairs just to the side of the door. Next to him sat a woman.

Introductions were made. The woman was Katherine, Walter's wife.

"You and Walter certainly were bikers," I said with admiration.

Katherine shrugged it off. "It was a lot of fun."

"Here's something you might like," Walter stated as he handed me an envelope. I opened it.

I looked inside. "Wow!" was all I was able to say.

Barbara leaned over to look. "Wow!" was all she was able to say.

Inside the envelope were a dozen or more 50's style small black and white photographs and a couple of color pictures. Several of the pictures were of Walter and his knucklehead. They showed a slender young man smiling broadly atop the Harley. Three pictures were of Katherine, Walter and the FL. On the back of each "AC Sep. '49" was written. There were two pictures of Walter's 1957 XL sportster. "That's a good looking bike," Barbara commented as she studied the picture.

There were a couple of pictures of Walter's other bikes. The 1981 sportster, the 1986 super glide and his last bike, the 1994 low rider. These were in color. One of Walter on the '81 sportster was taken at the entrance to Zion National Park. "We were there," I remarked. "Zion is beautiful," added Barbara.

When we finished looking at the pictures Barbara carefully put them back inside the envelope.

"Thank you for sharing your pictures with us," she commented as she handed Katherine the envelope.

"You're certainly welcomed," Katherine said with a laugh. Then she asked if we would do Walter a favor. Would we bring our bikes over to where "Walter could see them? He's been looking at them but he's too tired to walk across the parking lot."

Barbara and I quickly duck walked our bikes to a spot in front of Walter and Katherine. Then Barbara gave the run down on her 2007 sportster 1200R. She certainly knew her bike. When she finished I explained my 2007 super glide FXD.

Walter very much enjoyed our talks. He asked each of us questions, made comments. From the expression on his face Walter was in heaven. And a few minutes later as Barbara and I left the assisted living facility so were we.

Luck Would Have It

This story was told to me by my father-in-law. A more honest and trustworthy man I never met. He told it to me on a rainy summer night-just like the night this story took place.

Anyone with half a brain could have seen it coming. A dozen outlaw bikers and their molls drinking themselves blind and ingesting God only knows what illicit chemicals in a small out of the way bar. Within minutes of their uproariously loud entrance all the regular patrons had left through the back door.

The bar keep that night was an elderly man named Crepes. He wasn't a bartender by trade. He was doing the bar owner a favor by filling in for him until he returned from a wedding. Crepes had to leave by eleven thirty in order to get to his real job on time.

At first Crepes managed to keep the outlaws under control. However, he was quickly overwhelmed by the bikers. They urinated in the parking lot, broke beer pitchers, knocked over tables and fought amongst themselves. One particularly evil looking biker rode his motorcycle through the front door and did a burn out much to the amusement of his brother.

Fortunately for Crepes the bikers quickly tired of this small town establishment. With a final flourish of noise and violence they left. When the last outlaw, the same one who had ridden his bike inside the bar, roared out of the parking lot Crepes surveyed the damage they had wrought. Two tables and three chairs had their legs broken. Glass chards covered the floor next to one wall; the bikers had taken out their aggression by hurling pitchers against it. Every time a pitcher was smashed the bikers shouted the clubs name. It was a name Crepes would not forget. Nor would he forget that the bikers hadn't paid a dime for all the alcohol they drank.

When Ted, the bar's owner, walked through the front door Crepes was sweeping up the broken glass. The two life long friends just looked at each other. "I tried to call the police once they started getting out of control, but they threatened me," Crepes confessed, almost on the verge of tears. "I'm terribly sorry."

Ted knew there was nothing Crepes or anyone could have done in that situation. "It's okay," he told his good friend. "Now, you better get going. It's quarter after eleven, time for you to play God."

As I mentioned at the start of the story it was rainy night. Not a hard rain, more of a light drizzle. With a little more caution than usual one could safely ride a motorcycle on such a night. However, drunk and drugged outlaw bikers never use caution when riding their motorcycles. Not even on rain slick roads.

He was brought into the emergency room a few minutes after one in the morning. The rain soaked man was in critical condition. He had lain in a ditch for more than two hours. He had been accelerating to catch up with his club brothers when he lost control of his motorcycle and struck a tree.

None of the other outlaws noticed he was missing until they stopped for gas. The clubs president quickly surmised what had happened. He sent his men back the way they had just traveled. It was incredibly lucky that they found their injured brother. One of the outlaws' old ladies spotted a streak of red paint on the guard rail. The downed outlaw rode a red sportster.

It took the ambulance nearly twenty minutes to reach the site of the accident. The EMS quickly loaded the badly injured man into their vehicle. Then with one less than a dozen Harley's as escort the ambulance drove to the county hospital.

Edith, the admittance clerk, would not allow any of the bikers into the emergency room. "You can't go in there!" the heavy set woman sternly advised. When several of the outlaws tried to walk past her Edith stood in front of them. "There is a county sheriff inside the first room guarding a prisoner," she stated. "Do you want me to call for him?" Reluctantly one after another the outlaws went into the waiting room.

The man had lost too much blood and had too many injuries to be saved. He died within minutes of being brought into the emergency room. The nurses who had assisted the doctor were visibly distraught. For one young nurse this was her first patient who died. She was crying.

Before they left the room the doctor spoke to his team of nurses. He was an elderly doctor who had seen many die. He knew what the nurses were going through. "Each of you did your very best. Everything that could be done was done," he told them in his soft, soothing voice. Then turning to the young nurse he spoke these comforting words. "You're an excellent nurse and I'm proud to have you on my team."

The pretty blonde wiped away a tear. Then she smiled and whispered, "Thank you doctor Crepes."

Mike's Place

Mike didn't waste words, nor did he mince them. Someone once joked that he could have written the constitution on a paper napkin with space to spare. Mike was the owner and barkeep at a watering hole I happened upon a couple of summers ago. The two story red brick building was appropriately named Mike's Place.

Last year on a Saturday afternoon I stopped in for a beer. Mike's daughter was the waitress working that afternoon. Unlike her father, Cindy was outgoing, fast talking and very attractive.

After taking my order she went to a table where the only other customer sat. He was a heavy set outlaw with long hair and prison tattoos up and down both arms. He was making short work of polishing off a pitcher of suds. I had parked my sporty next to his ratty shovelhead.

When Cindy walked to the bar he watched her like a hungry hawk eyeing a fat mouse. Then he turned to me as he licked his lips. "Nice looking pussy," he remarked just loud enough for me to hear. Or so he thought.

Mike was out from behind the bar and standing over the outlaw in a flash. The big man was clearly angry.

"What did you just say?" he demanded.

The outlaw put his beer down then faced Mike. He instinctively knew that this was no man to screw with.

"I merely remarked that your waitress was pretty," he said lightheartedly. It was an obvious attempt to defuse an explosive situation. Mike pondered the mans answer.

"Here's my advise," the protective father stated forcefully, "keep your remarks to yourself." Before the one per center could answer Mike was back behind the bar.

The outlaw took a sip of his beer. Then he signaled for Cindy. The pretty blonde walked to his table under the watchful eye of her father. When she stopped he stood up. He looked her straight in the face. "I just want to apologize to you," he stated. "I am sorry."

A smile came over Cindy's face. "That's okay," she said. "I've heard worse." Then he dug into his pants and took out his wallet. From where I sat I could see that it was bulging with green backs. "Here," he said as he handed her a bill, "for the beer and your tip."

Cindy's eyes lit up when she studied the bill. "Fifty dollars," she remarked, "is too much," she exclaimed. They were the last words she ever spoke.

In a move so fast that it surely had to have been practiced the outlaw grabbed the bill from Cindy with one hand while the other went to the small of his back. When it came into view it held a small pistol. Cindy was so surprised that she didn't have time to react. He shot her in the mouth killing her instantly. Then he turned his attention to Mike. He fired once striking his victim in the chest. The fatally wounded man crashed to the floor. Four more bullets blazed across the room. The glass mirror behind the bar shattered. The gunman laughed. "I need to take better aim." Then as calmly as if he had ordered a happy meal the one per center walked out the door.

I was frantically punching 911 into my cell phone as he started his bike. I could barely hear the operator over the roar of the straight piped shovelhead.

"Quick! There's been a shooting!" I shouted into the midget phone.

Within minutes the police arrived. At least a dozen men in blue swarmed through the bar. Two took me aside and began questioning me. I gave them what information I could. It was the same information I had given the 911 operator. One late arriving sergeant broke down and cried when he saw Cindy's lifeless body. As another sergeant led him away I heard him tell the distraught policeman 'we'll get the bastard who murdered your niece and brother.'

The murderer was apprehended by an off duty cop at a gas station less than a mile from the bar. The newly minted officer had just heard about the shooting as he turned off his ignition to his jeep. He was going to drive to the crime scene when the biker matching the description given over the radio turned into the gas station. The heavy set man stopped at the pump behind the Jeep. The rookie smiled at his good fortune. Seconds later the outlaw shut off his bike. The cop jumped out of his vehicle. "Don't move!" he shouted with all the authority he could muster.

The outlaw reached for the gas pump. "Stop mother fucker!" the twenty two year old cop shouted.

The biker turned. Then in a most soothing voice stated, "To quote Robert Deniro 'are you talking to me?'" There was a look of total innocence on his bearded face.

The young cop was not fazed. "Here's a quote for you. Make one move and you're dead."

The outlaw smiled broadly. "And who said that?" he asked.

"I did asshole," the cop shot back.

This brought a chuckle from the outlaw. When the cop smiled the outlaw made his move. His right hand had just reached the handle of his pistol when the first of four bullets struck him. Two hit him in the chest and two in the stomach. The mortally wounded man reached for the gas pump, held onto it briefly. Then he staggered forward. "You lousy screw," he muttered. Then he closed his eyes and crumpled at the cop's feet.

In the year since I've turned the once barely holding it's own bar into a money maker. Wet t-shirt contests, good bands and cheap booze packs the customers in and the till ringing. Best of all my bro's like the place. It's too bad bro 'Tiny' had to pay with his life for the clubs new hangout. But what the hell, we did rename it "Tiny's Place.'

My Life

I came home from Vietnam in January 1972. As I had less than six months left on my enlistment the army gave me a choice. I could reenlist or I could be separated. I chose the latter option.

Three weeks after flying into Travis Air Force Base, California I was in a college classroom in New Jersey. It didn't take long to realize college life was for me. I took to it like a duck to water. My courses were for the most part interesting and well taught. I didn't have to work because the GI Bill and a 10% disability rating more than paid for everything. This allowed me to concentrate on my studies which I did. I intended to be the best history major I could be.

My college days were not entirely spent hitting the books. When they needed to be hit, I hit them. However, when I put them down I had fun. With the college population predominately female it was fairly easy to get a date. In no time I was dating two coeds. There was nothing serious nor did any of us expect anything to develop. We were just good friends who liked each other-a lot.

One Thursday afternoon in late March I was in the student center having a soda when a pretty blonde took a seat at the next table. Immediately she opened a book and started reading. I took a chance.

"Interesting book?" I asked.

The blonde put the book down. "Not in the least. American history," she explained.

"That hurts," I said in mock anguish.

"Oh. I'm sorry. I guess you're a history major."

I nodded my answer.

Cindy was a physical education major, a sneaker brain in the parlance of the student body. However, there was nothing sneakerish about her brain. It quickly became apparent that Cindy was a very intelligent young lady. She had graduated high school in three years, a fact that she was rightfully proud of.

I tried a little humor. "I too skipped a grade in high school."

Cindy was impressed. "What year?" She asked.

"My senior year." I answered.

A puzzled expression came over her fawn like face. Then she laughed. And when she laughed she reached out and touched my hand.

Cindy and I talked till she had to go to class. As she got up to leave I asked her out. The cute blonde smiled, said yes. She quickly wrote her address on a piece of paper.

"Saturday at noon," I called after her.

She smiled her consent.

When Cindy turned the corner I studied her address. She lived in Webster, a town I had driven through a hundred times. However, it had always been on the interstate. I had never been in the town.

The following morning Red, the Harley dealer I had corresponded with while in Vietnam, called. "We just got in a XLCH. It's blue. Do you want it?"

"Yes I do." I was barely able to contain myself.

"We're getting it ready now. Can you come in tomorrow?" Red asked.

I didn't have to think about it. "See you tomorrow."

"It'll be ready by noon."

"I'll be there at twelve sharp."

After I hung up the phone I shouted for the entire neighborhood to hear. Life was good, I thought. No, I corrected myself, life was very good.

It was a little after eleven when my father parked the Chevy in front of the Harley dealership. "Thanks for the lift dad." I said as I opened the car door. I hadn't taken two steps when my father called to me. I turned. "Drive carefully." He said. I nodded in agreement. "No sweaty da GI." I called back.

Red looked up from behind the counter when I walked through the door. "Your bike is in the back. It's all set to go," He stated, then quickly added, "You just have to sign some papers and then we need to go over the bike."

I followed him into his office. After we took our seats Red opened a drawer and took out a packet. Opening it he handed me the owners' manual. "Make sure you read it." He sternly advised. I started to glance through it when Red placed in front of me the first of many documents that needed my signature. After affixing my John Henry for the umpteenth time Red reached across the table. "The bike is yours." We shook hands.

We went into the back of the shop where the mechanics worked. Off in a corner my 'CH awaited me. I just wanted to get on it and ride. However, Red had different plans. He gave a very thorough class on the operations and mechanics of the bike. The long time Harley dealer left nothing to chance. When I fired it up, a task made easier by the heft of my jungle boots, we were both confident that I knew how to ride the 1000cc Harley.

It was with more than a bit of trepidation that I rode out of the shop. That feeling quickly went by the wayside. In no time I knew that this bike was made for me. The more I rode the more I wanted to get on the highway and crack open the throttle. However, I restrained my right wrist. "You have to break it in right," I kept telling myself. I stayed on the back roads where stop signs and traffic forced me to vary my speed and to shift often.

An hour or so later I put the kick stand down and pocketed the key. I had stopped at a popular diner which was often the scene of biker gatherings. Not only was I hungry I also needed a break. The cobra seat, though very stylish, was literally a pain in the ass.

There was a Harley dresser parked by the door of the diner. I stopped and checked it out. "Damn, that thing is big," I muttered to myself as I opened the door. No sooner had I entered the diner then a voice called to me.

"It's a real motorcycle."

I followed the voice to the booth nearest the cash register. It belonged to a man sitting by himself. His face was deeply tanned and weather beaten.

Not knowing how to respond I simply shrugged my shoulders. "Didn't say it wasn't."

"The way you were looking at it I figured you were riding a Honda. Then I saw your sportster." The weather beaten face smiled broadly. He motioned for me to join him.

"The name's Ken," he stated as he extended his hand. I shook it. "Peter," I responded.

Ken was a mailman and a dedicated biker. A fact that he readily admitted contributed to his divorce. "Once we had kids the wife didn't want to ride anymore. She was fearful of us getting into an accident and leaving the kids parentless. I should have listened." He paused, sipped his coffee. "Instead of parking the bike I rode it more."

He was about to start a sentence when the waitress came to our table. "More coffee?" she asked.

"No thank you." Ken answered.

The waitress turned her attention to me. "Coffee?"

"No. A chocolate shake, a hamburger well done and fries." The waitress nodded, scribbled on her pad.

Ken wasted no time. No sooner had the waitress left then he resumed telling me his life story.

"After the divorce I took a three week vacation and rode to California. Took me four days. I always wanted to ride the coast highway. And I did. Rode it from LA to San Fran. Now that's a great ride."

My lunch companion took a bite of his sandwich. "This place makes the best turkey sandwich." He commented. Then quickly continued where he had left off.

"I tell you this, California is the place. Ever been there?"

Before I could answer he continued. "Beautiful weather, great roads and beautiful women. Blonde, tanned and very friendly."

And at that exact instant I remembered a very friendly blonde a lot closer than California. Cindy. I frantically dug into my wallet for the piece of paper Cindy had given me. And as I unfolded it I prayed that it had her phone number on it. It did not. "Damn." I said through clenched teeth.

"Trouble?" Asked Ken who had only now stopped recounting a ride he had taken through the Arizona desert.

I nodded in the affirmative. "Yup. Trouble."

"What seems to be the matter?"

"I was supposed to be at a girls' house at twelve." I answered

Ken looked at his watch, let out a laugh. "You certainly missed that boat. And I guess you didn't write her phone number down." He took the piece of paper from my hand, studied it for a moment. Then he laughed.

"I give up. What's so funny?" I asked.

"Did you tell this young lady that you had a Harley?"

I nodded. "I'm pretty certain that I might have mentioned it." I confessed somewhat confused. Again that weather beaten face broke into a smile. A broad smile. His next question stumped me. "Can you remember a seven digit number?"

"Sure," I answered not knowing what he was getting at. Ken slowly said the numbers. Then he had me repeat them. Twice. Satisfied that I had memorized the numbers he reached into his pocket and pulled out a handful of change. He slid a quarter to me. "Go to the pay phone and dial that number. When Cindy answers tell her you were riding with me. My daughter will understand."

A True Brother

Having avoided what I considered to be the banal addictions of my fellow soldiers the three years I served in the army allowed me to accumulate a respectable bank account. This savings was only partially depleted by the purchasing of what the advertisers were then calling the night train, a 1971 Harley-Davidson super glide.

Financed by the generosity of those who worked I lived the good life. Rising late I would kick the shovelhead to life, don the mandatory helmet and ride to where ever the urge took me. Attached to the sissy bar was my sleeping bag and a bag with change of clothes, oil, tools and a few dollars

Mostly I rode alone. On occasion I did join one or two other bikers for jaunts of short duration. But anytime I went camping it was by myself. After years of community living I eschewed it in any form, no matter where it might show itself.

On one of my frequent trips to up state New York I steered the glide into the parking lot of a dimly lit nondescript diner. A few aging cars were clustered together in the gravel quadrangle. A small Honda motorcycle was parked under the street light just off to the side of the walk leading to the door of the Moonlight Restaurant.

My entrance into the small diner was barely acknowledged by any of the customers or by the tired waitress who sat at the counter with her back to me sipping coffee. I waited at the entrance as she lazily turned a page of the Inquirer, read a little, sipped her coffee, dragged on her cigarette, crushed it out. She rose, turned to me, smiled.

Gesturing for me to follow her I remained motionless, intending for her to savor the same derision that she had shown me.

An awkward moment of silence befell us. Again she gestured for me to follow her, again I moved not. "Ok. I apologize. It was rude of me to ignore you." Her voice was soft and easy, yet I discerned that it was also strained. Sensing that she was beaten long before this encounter I smiled, said a polite thank you and hoped that she would realize that I wanted a truce. She did.

A few hours later we sat opposite each other, a book and paper cluttered table between us. Linda drank her constant companion, coffee, I nursed a beer. The talk was light and easy. Before we realized how long we talked, yawns, first stifled, then open, became ever more common. "Hey you better start for home. You'll fall asleep at the wheel. Or should I say at the handle bars?" We both laughed as I picked up my jacket and helmet.

"She's a pretty level headed chick," I thought to myself as I drove down the Palisades Interstate. Mulling over our conversation I began to realize that Linda Zenbowski was not only endowed with a traditional education but that she also had plenty of common sense. She also had more than her share of bad luck. Having worked her way through college in three and one half years while maintaining a B plus average she also had the time to volunteer in a hospital and still work part time at the Moonlight. But then her father became ill, requiring constant medical attention, and there went Linda's savings. Now instead of pursuing her masters she was working as a waitress who at best could only make token payments on her fathers ever increasing medical bills. No wonder she appeared beaten! And then I come along and gave her a hard time.

Within a week of Linda and I having met her father died. Together we went to his funeral. The morning of the internment was chilly with over cast skies and rain predicted. Linda dressed in black as did her younger sister Jeanette and their mother. Mrs. Zenbowski, a kindly gray haired woman whom I had met twice before, carried the bible from which thirty two years earlier her and Mr. Zenbowski were married.

After that bleak day Linda became increasingly more dependant on me. She wanted to be taken where ever I went and sensing her loneliness I took her along. She stood with me in the unemployment line, waited patiently for me as I interviewed for jobs, rode with me to the Harley shop for a quart of oil. Then late in an evening that had seen me consume far too much beer, Linda still quite sober, began to talk of our relationship in terms far different than those that I would describe it with. Though drunk and barely able to talk the shattering effect of her words awoke me instantly.

We argued that night. I slurred my words, she pleaded for quiet so that she might speak the words that would change my mind. I was adamant, she was perstiant and early the next morning I staggered to my Harley while Linda called to me from the porch.

"Forget it!" I shouted above the roar of the 74. The clutch was released, the throttled rolled and half blinded by Budweiser's off I went.

I had just crossed into Jersey when the headlights appeared in my mirror. The brisk air had brought my dulled senses to life and I could tell that the car was traveling at a good rate of speed. I watched in fascination as the two lights grew larger and larger in my mirror. Then I watched in horror as the headlights turned into my lane.

The lolloping shovelhead was dropped a gear, the throttle opened fully. The engine screamed, fourth gear was kicked in, the speedometer showed 85. I turned and looked into the grim face of Linda, now not more than ten feet behind me and gaining!

There was only one chance for me to escape the deadly Pontiac. An exit ramp a few seconds further down the highway beckoned to me. But could I make it? And if I could would the GTO merely follow suit and crush me on some side street? But there was no other choice; I had to go for it. At the last split moment of time threw the glide into a hard right turn. The pipes scrapped and I fought her over still more. The curve of the ramp came up; the glide was thrown down to the left. The brakes were mashed, I hung on tight and at 80 I went through the stop sign.

I never looked back, only glanced once at the interstate. Linda's car was nowhere to been. Traveling as fast as she was she was far gone. The remaining miles home were traveled on back roads. When I reached home I rode the glide up the driveway, dismounted, opened the garage door, rode the bike in, shut if off, closed the door, locked it. Then I went into the house, went upstairs to the bathroom and vomited.

A few days later I began working for my brother who was the senior partner in a two man construction company. The work was hard and the pay was low, but fortunately I remained on unemployment and was thus able to continue living comfortably.

It was a cool Saturday evening. A foxy young lady and I had ridden most of the afternoon and now having eaten a fine Italian meal we sought a night spot for dancing. Not being familiar with the neighborhood that we found ourselves in I pulled into a large gas station and asked the pimply faced teenager at the pump where there might be a bar. With wiping rag in hand he pointed to a multi colored building a short distance down the highway, a building that Nancy and I were soon sitting on the glide in front of.

"What do you think?" asked the wispy haired blonde. The roar of the engine was her answer. I found an empty spot to park next to a much chromed sportster.

Laughing we climbed the stairs that lead to the Bedlam of the Highway. Suddenly a sickening feeling of doom came over me. Not knowing what had caused such an omen I stopped. Turning I saw the reason for my sickening feeling. A green GTO, barely visible from where we now stood, invisible from where we had parked, caught my eye. The sight of which sent the chilling memory of a night of terror racing through my body. The two headlights, the grim face, the near suicidal exit off a darkened highway. It all came back, thank you Linda Zenbowski.

Uttering a not so silent curse I left a startled Nancy, went to the GTO and promptly let the air out of all four tires. Then enjoining a confused fox to join me I quickly brought the shovelhead to life and over the protests of a helmet less Nancy I headed out of the lot. As I shifted into second gear, a compulsory last look at the bar brought fear to me. On the steps that only minutes before I had paused upon Linda now stood.

The following Monday at work lunch couldn't come fast. The weather was miserable, hot and humid, and the work was back breaking. Around quarter after twelve my brother and his partner put down their tools and got in the truck. "We have to go to the lumber yard. We'll stop and pick up lunch, in the mean time keep working."

As soon as the over loaded pick up turned the corner I sat down and there I remained till the sound of squealing tires wakened me from my daydream. Believing that my brother had returned with lunch I rose. However instead of looking at a hamburger I was facing a gun totting Linda Zenbowski.

"You bastard you! Letting the air out of my tires! I should have killed you when I had the chance. No, I let you go and what do you do? You bastard!"

I stood mute, transfixed. Ever closer she came. Her profanity continued, becoming more vile and louder as she neared me. There was nothing I could do. Her eyes were filled with the hate that transforms itself into the act of murder. I had seen that look once before. In Viet Nam, after a fierce fire fight, a young soldier had found the mutilated body of his friend. His eyes had become glazed and from his mouth froth did show, as did froth now show on the corners of Linda's mouth and her eyes were as that soldiers eyes had been.

"You bastard you!" screamed the hysterical woman.

I trembled in fear and saw not past the figure before me. So paralyzed was I that my eyes could only stare blankly into the eyes of my murderer.

"You stinkin . . ." Bam! "aagh."

She died before my eyes, a nail studded board smashed into her head. My brother had returned with our lunch.

A cold ride to a warm welcome

Last night was cold, windy and darker than an ex-wife's heart. November in the northeast. A perfect night to spend curled up in front of a roaring fire with a brunette and a bottle of brandy.

Though I wouldn't mind having a little R&R with a certain brunette I know, last night was also a good night for a ride. Not a perfect night. Just a good night. And that's about all the incentive I need to get on my bike.

I didn't have a destination in mind. I just wanted to ride. Snow could come any day so this just might be my last putt of the year. The low rider had a full tank of gas and I had a few bucks in my wallet. What more do you need?

For the first ten or fifteen miles I stuck to back roads. Took it nice and easy. Pulled over a couple of times too. Letting the engine warm up. When the Dunlop's finally hit the interstate the evo was running strong. I enjoy riding the super slab. No traffic lights, no stop signs and everybody going in the same direction. Once in fifth gear the feet went to the highway pegs and I settled in for the duration.

The only part of my body that was cold was my finger tips. Not terribly cold. Just an annoyance. One I could live with. The rest of me was fine. Traffic was light, the Harley was rumbling and life was good.

I stayed on the interstate for nearly an hour. Got off a few miles from the GW Bridge which would have taken me across the Hudson to the big tomato. I certainly didn't want to ride in that mad house, tonight or any other night. I was about to get back on I-80 west bound when I spotted a most inviting sign. It was in the window of a nondescript brick building near the on ramp. "Cold Beer," it proudly proclaimed. How could anyone, I ask you, pass by such effective advertising?

It took my eyes a moment to adjust to the bars darkness. When I was able to see I looked the place over. There were half a dozen or so men and a couple of women scatted among the four or five tables and booths. At the bar two guys joked loudly. Both wore Harley T-shirts. A guy and his very jovial and quite plump female friend were shooting a game of straight on the lone pool table. Next to the bathroom the juke box was blaring out a Doobie Brothers song. There were cigarette butts on the floor and the air was filled with the aroma of smoke and alcohol. No two ways about it, the joint was a dive. My kind of place. I felt right at home. Unzipping my leather jacket I sat my ass on a stool at the bar.

"What'll have?" asked the barkeep in a deep Irish brogue. He could have come right out of central casting. Red hair, ruddy complexion. Stocky. Bulging forearms. One with a tattoo. "USMC RVN '69" He looked capable of mixing one potent drink or delivering a killer punch. And probably didn't care which you got.

"A Bud," I stated, putting a ten dollar bill down. The barkeep nodded, poured me a glass of the second best thing to come out of Milwaukee. Make that the third best thing to come of Milwaukee. There was this blonde who, but that's another story. I took a drink. Good. To paraphrase a former governor of our great state, 'cold beer and you. Perfect together.'

"You ride?" a voice from the end of the bar called. Without turning I gave my answer.

"That I do."

Silence.

"What ya ride?" the inquiring voice wanted to know.

I took a sip of beer. Turned. The voice belonged to one of the guys at the bar. A rail thin man about thirty. Hard to tell. With his unkempt shoulder length hair and scraggly beard and mustache he could have been five years younger or twenty years older. Or he could have been Mr. Death himself. Somewhat of a scary looking individual.

"A 1992 low rider," I stated matter of fact.

He nodded his head, took a drag off his cigarette. A moment of silence. "Evo," he spits out. Made it sound like a deadly disease. Sorry to tell you, but you ain't going to make it. You got evo.

"Rides a new evo," he related with relish to his friend. They chuckled at their private joke.

"Yeah. A new evo," I state forcefully. Then quickly added with derision, "parked it next to your '50 pan. You know, the one you ride in year dreams." I went back to my beer. Tasted good. So good in fact that without further ado I polished off the rest of the glass. Then I pocketed my bills and got up to leave. And I would have too. However, she walked through the door.

She stood about five four. Couldn't have weighed more than one twenty. Her wispy blonde hair cascaded over her shoulders. She wore skin tight jeans and a loose denim jacket over a white T-shirt. Clothes that were meant to show off her tight, lithe body. And they did. However, what caught my eye and made me grin were the sunglasses she was wearing. They were so black superman couldn't see through them. And he has x-ray vision. If Mr. Webster ever needs to put a person next to the word sassy, here she is.

For a long moment we just stood and looked at each other. She broke the silence. "You can move out of my way now." Spoken like a true JAP.

I chuckled, stepped aside. "Would you like a beer?" I asked. She titled her head checked me over. Smiled with just the corner of her lips. "Sure." She said it in a voice filled with a lack of emotion. We slid into a booth. No sooner did we get comfortable then the two jerks at the bar casually strolled over to us.

"Cindy," the talkative one begins, "now I've known Roger for only 20 years, so I don't know him as well as you know him." He gestures to me with his hand. "So pardon me if I say this guy don't look like the Roger I know." He punctuates his remarks with a belch. His partner snickered, took a long hit of courage from his glass.

I guess Cindy didn't care for these two guys anymore than I did. In a not very subtle way she basically told the dynamic duo to have sex with themselves and that she'd do whatever the hell she felt like doing. To make certain that there was no misunderstanding her feelings she slid her arms around my neck, leaned forward and gave me one hell of a kiss. After that things got pretty wild pretty fast.

Our two friends didn't take to Cindy's public display of affection. And I certainly didn't appreciate having my head snapped back by my ponytail. My tormenter started to snarl something, however, he never finished his sentence. I came across with the hardest right I ever threw-in or out of the ring. Caught him in the solar plexus, doubling him over in pain. A second punch, another right, this one to the nose sent him stumbling backwards. I stood up and hit him with a left that sent him crashing to the floor. His startled partner could only take a deep breath and curse me. With as friendly a smile as I could muster I asked him if he would to step up to the place. "Or are you chicken?" I goaded him with a laugh.

He wasn't chicken. That much I got to give him. Stupid? Yes. But not chicken. If I hadn't seen it myself I might not believe what he did. Lets out a primeval scream, puts his head down and charged. He didn't have a chance. Instinctively I stepped aside and nailed him with a round house kick to the face. He dropped in his tracks like a sack of cement.

The bartender didn't call the cops. He casually walked over to the booth, studied my handiwork. "They got what they were looking for," was all he remarked. He turned his attention back to the two men on his floor. Both were bent over in pain. The first guy down was spitting up his guts while his partner was trying to stop a profusely bleeding nose and mouth. He held two of his teeth in one hand. Without bending over the barkeep asked if they wanted him to call an ambulance. They didn't. "Good. Now get up and get out of here." He told them. Then he went back behind the bar as if nothing had happened.

I turned to Cindy who had remained seated during the fight. "Let's get on my bike and leave. I got another helmet."

Without hesitation she answered. And not exactly the words I wanted to hear. "I'm meeting my boyfriend here. He should be coming any minute."

I was stunned. What's with this girl, I wondered. Then it came to me. I reached over and took off her sunglasses. I looked deep into her lovely but incredibly sad face. She used a lot of make up. She should have used more. Her bruises were still visible. Poor girl, I thought.

I gently slid the sunglasses back over her eyes and onto her nose. "You should get away from him. One day he's going to more than hurt you," I told her. She softly nodded in agreement. "I know," she answered in a whisper, "but I can't." She quickly took a drink from her beer.

Without another word I walked out the door. The ride home was uneventful. However, the moment I parked the scooter in the garage the first snow of the year began to fall.

Three Fat Pigs

I caught sight of them in my mirror as they entered the interstate. There were three of them, all dressers. Their unmistakable batwing fairings told me they were Harleys.

The first was besides me in a flash. I glanced to my left just as the black Electra Glide passed me. I nodded to the rider; he was like a statue starring straight ahead. No sooner had he completed his pass then the second dresser made his move. Again I nodded; again the rider stared straight ahead.

I looked in my left mirror expecting to see the third bike start its pass. I should have looked in the other mirror. The red Harley roared past me on my right and in my lane! I doubt more than three inches separated his fairing and my handlebar. No make that an inch.

"Asshole!" I shouted at the top of my lungs. I knew he couldn't hear me but I figured he might see me giving him the finger. He did. He returned the gesture. Then he fell in behind his two companions as casually as if he had no idea that he had nearly caused an accident.

A massive dose of adrenaline shot through my veins. My heart raced a mile a minute and crazy thoughts flashed through my mind. Open up the sportster and catch the jerk and force him to a stop. Pass him in his lane and see how he likes it. Accelerate ahead of him and then don't let him pass.

Instead I took a deep breath and backed off the throttle. A minute or two later I regained my composure. As the sporty started up a hill I slowly brought the speed back to seventy. At the crest I spotted three black dots disappearing in the distance.

The rest of the ride to my sister's apartment for her birthday party went without incident. It was just another boring ride on the super slab.

Cindy met me at the door. She was wearing a Harley halter top and jean shorts. As we hugged I noted the slender blondes' deep tan. "Must be nice having the summers off so you can lay out by the pool and tan all day," I remarked as we separated. Cindy had just finished her first year teaching elementary school. "It must be nice," the sassy blonde snapped back, "to ride a new Harley and not have student loans to pay off." We both laughed.

I wished her a happy twenty third then handed her her birthday card. "Sorry about it being beat up, it was strapped to my sissy bar," I explained as she opened the dog eared card. When she finished reading it a smile flashed across her face. "That was very cute," she said with a laugh, "you writing, 'to the best sister I have.' I am your only sister!"

Cindy and I have always had a special relationship. We were more than brother and sister. We were friends. In high school I beat a kid to a pulp because he had started a rumor about her. The following day he apologized to her. Cindy repaid the favor many times over by setting me up with her friends. I have to admit it; I have some very fine memories of a cheerleader she set me up with.

"Where's everybody else?" I wondered.

Cindy smiled impishly. "I told them to come at four."

"Why?"

"Why did I tell everyone but you that the party started not at one but at four? Because I have a surprise for you," Cindy said excitedly. She hurried to the kitchen. When she returned she held a letter and an envelope. She handed me the envelope. "Read it," Cindy advised me. The return address was a lawyer's office half way across the country.

"What is this?" I asked with a puzzle look on my face.

"It came in the mail Monday or Tuesday. I thought it was just some more legal papers. All I've been doing since the funerals is filling out forms and talking with lawyers. Mom and dad had a lot of insurance policies. I figured this was another form letter for me to fill out. It isn't. Read it."

Cindy placed the letter in my hand. I read it. It was brief and to the point. Then I reread it.

"I couldn't believe it either!" Cindy exclaimed.

For a moment I was in a state of disbelief. "It's true?"

"It's true," Cindy assured me. "I spoke with the lawyer yesterday."

"It's for real?" I asked, still not believing what I had just read.

Cindy nodded her head. "It's true. It's true." She repeated.

Slowly it dawned on me. I smiled broadly. So did Cindy. Sliding her hand in mine she whispered, "Let's do it."

"Let's do what?" I asked.

Cindy was direct. "Let's screw our unrelated brains out."

As we walked to her bedroom I dropped the letter. The letter which stated I had been adopted.

They looked every inch

One was tall and muscular. The other was of average height and pot bellied. One was long haired and unshaven. The other was bald and clean shaven. One was heavily inked. The other was sans tattoo. One looked every inch the bad assed biker. The other looked every inch the insurance salesman.

Tim Bolton and Dave Wright had ridden their bikes across Texas and New Mexico to this one pump gas station in the Arizona desert. It was there that Bolton's Honda wouldn't start.

"Your bike decided to take a shit again," Wright dryly remarked. His cracked lips showed but the slightest trace of a smile.

"Fuck you!" snapped Bolton as he frantically pressed on the starter button. Then he stomped repeatedly on the kicker arm. Not a sound did the engine make.

"That's funny," Wright said with a laugh, "my Harley just keeps on running." He revved the engine. "See, I told you so."

"For the umpteenth time," Bolton snarled, "fuck you and fuck that Harley you're riding." The big man continued his futile attempts to bring his 250 to life. Frustrated beyond belief he began to sweat. "Fuck! Fuck! Fuck!" he repeated again and again.

Wright smiled. "You better watch your language," he said in as soothing voice as he could manage. "You don't want to scare off the young lady."

The lean and long legged blonde giggled when she saw Bolton on his Honda. "My, that is a nice motorcycle," she teased, "does your

grand mother know you borrowed her bicycle, I mean motorcycle?"
The blonde and Wright laughed and laughed.

Then she turned to Wright. "I sure would like to go for a ride
on your Harley and then have sex," the blonde squealed. Wright
gestured to the low rider's passenger seat which the blonde promptly
threw a leg over. When she sat down Wright called to Bolton. "Now
don't you go anywhere," he said with a smile worthy of a tooth paste
commercial.

A second later the blonde called to Bolton. "We won't be gone
long. I'm going to have him drive us to the park at the end of the
street. Then I'm going to give him the best blow job in the world."
As the Harley sped off she blew Bolton a kiss.

Minutes later Wright's Harley screeched to a stop next to Bolton's
Honda. Wright had the look of complete satisfaction on his face. So
did the blonde.

The blonde got off the bike. "That was incredible," she not
so quietly whispered into Wrights ear. When she realized that she
said it loud enough for Bolton to hear her she laughed. "Why
should I whisper?" she asked rhetorically. Turning to Bolton she
continued. "I just had the best sex of my life!" Bolton stared at her
in disbelief.

The two bikers watched as the blonde walked across the parking
lot. And they could hear her say over and over, "I just had the best
sex of my life!"

When she disappeared from sight Wright called to his traveling
companion. "I think your bike will start now."

Methodically Bolton turned out the kicker arm. No sooner did
he place his boot on it then the two stroke Honda came to life. In
seconds Bolton and bike were enveloped in a cloud of blue smoke.

"Why don't we ride the interstate for a while?" Wright suggested
knowing full well that Bolton had no choice but to follow. Still the
Honda rider protested. But all in vain, minutes later the Honda
followed the Harley up the onramp and onto the super slab.

The stroked low rider accelerated hard. Then Wright casually
steered it into the fast lane which was completely empty of vehicles.
The anemic Honda frantically tried to get up to speed to enter the
slow lane. However, an endless procession of double tandem 18
wheelers kept him on the shoulder.

Wright stretched his legs to the highway pegs and leaned back against his duffel bag. He had smooth sailing on his ribbon of blacktop.

Bolton had to fight with all his might to keep from being blow over by the passing big rigs. He also had to continuously dodge the debris that was scattered up and down the shoulder.

Wright happened to glance at Bolton the instant a speeding 18 wheeler missed crushing the Honda and it's rider by inches. Wright laughed when he saw the sheer terror on Bolton's face.

Tiring of riding Wright exited the interstate followed by one stressed out Honda rider. The Harley stopped at the bottom of the off ramp. Seconds later the Honda pulled along side him.

"I'm hungry and thirsty," Wright announced. "What do you say we get something to eat and a couple of cold beers to wash it down?"

Before the Honda rider could answer the low rider sped across the street into the parking lot of a steak house. Seconds later Wright and a guy riding a sportster were backing their bikes into a parking space next to the entrance. "Perfect timing," the XL rider stated as they shut off their bikes. When Bolton tried to park his Honda next to the two Harley's the sportster rider would have none of it. "Park your Jap piece of shit in Tokyo!" he barked. Bolton meekly shifted into gear and rode away. The two Harley riders laughed heartily.

The waitress was young and pretty. "We have the best steak you'll ever eat," she proclaimed with a smile.

"Then that's what I'll have," Wright laughed.

"Me too," Bolton seconded.

The waitress went to the kitchen and immediately returned with Wright's order.

"Where's mine?" a perplexed Bolton asked as she placed the huge steak in front of the Harley rider.

The waitress giggled. "The dog ate it."

"Well then," Bolton demanded, "cook another one."

The cute blonde again giggled. "We're all out of everything. Sorry." She turned and went back to the kitchen. A moment later she came forth with a great big steak.

"That's more like it," Bolton exclaimed. Unfortunately for him the waitress went to the table where the sportster ride sat.

"What is going on here?" Bolton demanded.

Again the waitress giggled. "The cook found one more steak," she answered as she walked past the Honda rider.

Bolton was speechless. However, Wright was not. "That was the best steak I ever ate. I'm stuffed." He stood up to leave. "What do you say we call it a day? Check into a hotel and relax." Bolton didn't answer, not that it mattered. Like a shadow he followed the Harley riding insurance salesman.

The two men approached the clerk behind the counter. Each stated that they would like a room for the night.

"Aren't you the lucky one!" exclaimed the clerk as he turned to Wright. "We just had a cancellation by a man named Wright. So I guess you didn't cancel after all." Both men laughed. "And best of all," continued the clerk, "the room is the presidential suite."

The clerk signaled for a bell boy to take Wright's luggage to his room. Wright followed the young boy to the elevator which opened the second they approached it.

"And what about me?" asked a dejected and exhausted Bolton.

The clerk smiled broadly. "What do you mean?"

"Everywhere I go I get treated like I don't matter."

The clerk listened intently as Bolton went on and on. The Honda rider recapped all the days' events. When he finished the clerk's smile disappeared. In its place was as hard a look as ever seen by man.

"Don't you remember?" the clerk asked as he got eye ball to eye ball with Bolton.

"Remember what?" Bolton whimpered.

"You were a bike thief."

Bolton shrugged his shoulders. "So what?" he asked.

"Were is the key word here," the clerk explained. "You're dead. And this is hell. Get used to it, this is your eternity."

Twenty years on the road

I've been on the road more than 20 years. In my travels I've come in contact with many people. Most have been good and decent people. Some have been true friends. And some have been real shit heads.

Most of the latter group have been men in blue uniforms who carry guns and work for some level of government. I'm not saying every cop is a shit head. There have been one or two who fall into the good and decent category. Unfortunately, they have been the exception. Most cops that I've had contact with are shit heads.

Now don't make me out to be some bad assed biker. I'm certainly not. My hair is short, I'm clean shaven and I ride a stock 1981 Sturgis. About the only crime I'm guilty of is every once in a while opening up the old shovelhead. Let me tell you those eighty cubes can still pull pretty good!

Right about now you're probably wondering why would a cop, any cop, screw with me. Good question. I guess we'll have to let the man in blue who just pulled me over answer that question.

"Do you know why I stopped you?" He asks in a voice void of pitch.

"No, sir." I wait expecting to be told the reason why but he doesn't answer. A moment later he's looking at my bike like he was studying it. I clear my throat.

He quickly turns his attention back to me. "License, registration and proof of insurance," he quickly asks.

Not wanting to get shot I explain to the officer that "my wallet is in my left rear pocket. In order for me to get it I'm going to have to stand up." He nods his approval. "Go ahead," he states in that vapid voice of his. I stand up and retrieve my wallet. Though I've gotten things out of it a hundred times today I fumble getting the documents out. When I finally hand them to the officer he's grinning. "A little nervous?"

"No sir, just klutzy." I explain.

The cop glances at my documents than hands them back to me. "Everything seems to be in order," he states. Again I fumble with my wallet. No sooner do I sit down when the cop walks to the front of the bike. I watch as he looks over the front fork.

"Sturgis!" He exclaims. "This is a 1981 Sturgis." He evidently can read the decal on the fork cover.

"Yes, it is," I state. My answer brings a 'wow' from the cop. Smiling ear to ear he comes along side me.

"My dad had a '81 Sturgis," he excitedly tells me. "It was black, just like yours."

"Black and orange," I correct him. "Let's not forget the orange."

The cop laughs. "That's right. Black and orange. Harley's colors." He walks to the right side of the bike.

"You still have the stock air cleaner and pipes." I cannot tell whether it's a question or a statement.

"Stock as the day I bought it," I inform him.

After a pause he asks, "How long have you owned it?"

"I bought if new." Again he lets out with a 'wow.'

"Does your father still have his?" I ask.

Instantly the cops face saddens. "He was killed on it."

"I'm sorry for your loss," I tell him. For a moment there was silence. Then he broke it. "Dad was a bus driver. He worked the midnight to eight shift. He had just gotten work when a drunk driver rear ended him. It was his birthday that day."

What do you say after that? Again there was silence. And again he broke it with yet another 'wow.' "Today is the seventh. Today would have been dad's 51st birthday."

"Do you have many memories of him?" I asked.

"Some. I was only eight years old. I still remember dad taking me for a ride around the lake on the bike. And him and I cleaning it. I have a picture of dad and me on the bike in my wallet." Now it was his turn to fumble with his wallet.

"A little nervous?" I asked. The cop looked at me and smiled.

"There," he stated handing me the picture.

I studied it for a good minute. "This is a nice picture," I told him. "A very nice picture."

"I'm fond of it," the cop stated as he put the photo back in his wallet. His eyes were welled up and I could tell he was on the verge of crying.

"What about the Yankees winning again," I quickly stated.

The cop swallowed, rubbed his eyes then smiled. "Yeah," he said, "the Yankees win again."

A minute later he was walking back to his patrol car. As he opened the door he turned and called to me. "You take it easy," he advised.

"You too," I called back as I brought the Sturgis to life.

When he pulled along side me I signaled for him to roll down the passenger side window.

He did.

"I bet your mother would love to hear from you today. Remembering your dad's birthday would mean a lot to her."

The cop nodded. "It would. Thanks." The window started rising.

"And," I called, "your little sister Linda would love a phone call too. You know how sad she gets every year."

Again the cop nodded. Then he accelerated onto the highway. It wasn't until he got up to speed that he realized he had never mentioned to the biker that he had a little sister named Linda.

I knew my last statement would stick in his mind. That he'd replay our encounter again and again. And everytime he'd be damned trying to figure out when he said anything about Linda.

But why shouldn't I mention Linda? Afterall she is my daughter.

A happy ending

$\overline{}$

Mike was an alcoholic. Everyone knew it. For years his friends had watched him stumble out of bars and get on his bike. More than a few times Mike was too drunk to start his super glide. On those occasions the bear like man would slide off his 74 and sleep on the pavement besides it.

However, most nights Mike was able to start his shovelhead. Then with great fanfare he'd roar off into the night. Many of his take offs were sans lights. And of course he never wore a helmet even though the law required it.

Cindy, Mike's sometimes girl friend, speculated that a guardian angel rode with him. "There is no other explanation," she stated, "as to how night after night he makes it safely to his apartment." When Mike left a bar he was usually so drunk that even an avowed atheist could believe Cindy's theory.

Many of Mike's friends tried to get him to slow down. "Why don't you take it easy tonight and go for a ride?" they'd suggest. Or "let's go down to the park and watch the ball games." Like most alcoholics Mike wouldn't be detoured from his routine.

"Screw taking it easy," he would shoot back, "I'm going for a ride alright, right down to DK's." That's the hole in the wall bar where Mike does most of his drinking. And his come back to the second suggestion was just as curt. "I can watch the games at DK's. They got a good tv there."

Now you may be wondering why anyone would give a damn about an anti-social drunk who seemed intent on killing himself. The

197

reason is simple. Mike had friends, lots of friends, partly because he was a good guy and partly because he had money. Lot's of money.

Years ago Mike had invested in a tech company. Like many tech companies at first the stock shot through the roof. Then in a move that could also be attributed to the intervention of his guardian angel Mike sold every share he owned. People thought he was nuts. Two weeks later the company went bust. It was estimated that Mike banked anywhere from seven to nine million big ones. However large the amount it was more than enough to finance his nightly binges.

Mike knew his money was the reason why he was so popular at DK's. "I may be a drunk," he confessed more than once, "but I'm not an idiot. I know who my real friends are." His real friends cared about him. They were the ones who tried to get him to take a ride or to spend an evening watching the kids play ball.

They remember him when he was a hard working plumber. They remember him when he started his own business. They remember him the day he married his high school sweet heart. And they remember him the day his world came crashing down.

It was a Monday in October when Mike's wife left him. The note was short and to the point. "I'm not going to spend my life as the wife of a plumber." That's all she had written. She didn't even sign it. Mike found it on the kitchen table.

Mike got drunk that night. The next morning he got up and went to work. He still had a business to run and customers to service. As I said, he was a hard worker. However, little by little he began to change. He started to spend less time on the job and more time at DK's. His work suffered and he lost customers. The final straw was when he cashed in his stocks. He sold his equipment for pennies on the dollar and took up residence on the end barstool at DK's.

No one thought Mike would live to see his thirtieth birthday. We all figured his drinking would kill him long before then. But he surprised us all. Mike lived to enjoy the party Cindy threw to celebrate his turning the big three o.

Cindy had rented the town hall and hired a band. There was plenty of food and lots of soda. She had invited only the people who were close to Mike before the fall. To make certain no free loaders from DK's got in Cindy had hired a bouncer to keep watch at the door. "If they aren't on the list," she instructed the former college linemen, "don't let them in."

Cindy meant a lot to Mike. They had gone out a couple of times. However, Cindy would not tolerate his drinking. "It's either me or the booze," she warned him. "You drink, I'm gone." She even got him to attend an AA meeting.

Mike would stop drinking for a day or two, then he'd fall back into its clutches. True to her word, Cindy would pack her things and leave. But Cindy never gave up on Mike. She would hurry across town whenever he needed her.

The birthday boy had been sober two days the day of the party. When he rode up on his bike he was hardly recognizable. For one thing he was wearing a helmet. And he was clean shaven and wearing neatly pressed pants, a button down shirt and tie and shoes that were shined. I couldn't help but whistle when he walked up to me.

"Who the duck are you?" I laughed as we shook hands.

My life long friend clasped my hand firmly. "I'm starting over," he stated with a smile. He sounded very serious so I kept quiet. "I'm giving up the old life," he continued. "I realize that people, my true friends, have been trying to help me. I'm doing this for everyone who has stood by me."

"I'm happy for you," was all I could think of to say.

Still clasping my hand Mike told me how much he appreciated all that I had tried to do for him. Then he went on to say he was going to ask Cindy to marry him. I was speechless.

Just as his words were beginning to sink in Mike muttered something, turned and began walking to his bike. "I'll be right back," he called over his shoulder. They were the last words he ever spoke.

I guess it's ironic that Mike would be killed by a drunk driver.

It Shows

I've been going to the gym religiously for the past year and a half. Three days a week I'm lifting weights like a maniac. On my off days I swim. Lap after endless lap. It sounds boring and it is, however, it's increased my endurance tremendously. And that has helped me lift more. I'm not only getting strong I'm also feeling better and looking better to boot. What I got going is a win-win situation.

This past Saturday I woke up feeling stronger and more energetic than usual. Grabbing my helmet and keys I told myself that not only would I swim I'd also lift. That feeling didn't leave me even though I took an hour long ride before parking my sporty at the gym.

I had just started curling when she stepped onto the treadmill closest to me. She was a very pretty young lady. Tall, slender, tanned and blonde; she radiated good health. In her pink sneakers, blue shorts and white t-shirt she was the very picture of the quintessential California girl.

When I picked up the curling bar for my second set I could not help but notice that she had taken her eyes off the overhead television and was looking at me. I nodded to her and to my surprise she smiled. My heart rate jumped. I did an extra rep and told myself to screw swimming.

My mind raced as I did my second set. Why was she smiling at me? Could it be that she found me attractive? Or was it because I was wearing a Harley t-shirt and she had seen my 1200 in the parking lot? Whatever her reason I intended to find the answer.

After my third and final set of curls my biceps were on fire. As I started for the water fountain she caught my attention. She was waving to me in a funny sort of way. This was the opening I was looking for. I walked over to her.

"Hello," I said with a smile.

The young lady wiped her brow and smiled.

I started to say something when she asked the oddest question. "Is that bracelet from Vietnam?" She pointed to my left wrist.

"Yes it is," I answered. I was impressed. She was the first person ever to know that.

Then she wiggled her hand the way she had moments earlier. A bronze ring slid down her arm.

"Just like yours," stated the perspiring blonde as she began twirling the ring in her fingers.

"Yes, it is," I commented. Both rings looked identical.

"Where did you get your ring?" she asked with the innocents of a doe.

I took a deep breath before answering. "Vietnam."

"I thought so," she replied with certainty.

Then she said the words I dreaded to hear.

"That's where my grandfather got this ring."

Last Ride

It was to be my last ride of the year. Winter was here and so was the end of my motorcycle insurance coverage. After today I'd have to be satisfied with memories and plans for the spring.

"You have to be nuts," I thought to myself as I sat on the idling super glide. Even dressed like the Michelin man in leathers I was cold. And I wasn't even moving!

I felt the rocker boxes to make sure they were warm. Satisfied, I flipped down my face shield, engaged first gear and was off. By the time I reached the end of the block I was ready to call it quits. Then I thought, 'this is the last time you'll ride till who knows when.' I turned the corner and gunned the Harley.

I have always enjoyed interstate riding so that's where I headed. Traffic was light on I-78 which was good. Frozen as I was I didn't want to have to move around any. I kept the super glide in the right lane at the posted speed limit. Whenever a car passed me the occupants would stare at me like I was nuts. There they were in cars with the heater going full blast and I'm riding a bike. And smiling. I'd give each and every car the biggest smile possible. However, after not many miles that smile became a frozen sneer. Man it was cold!

About 20 miles down the road I called it quits. The cold was too much for me. The ride back was even worse then the ride going. Those smiles I had given to car drivers were but a memory. All I wanted to do was get back inside my house. My warm house. I nudged the twin cam up to 80 and prayed that a cop wouldn't stop me. The thought of stopping and then having to start moving all over again in this cold wasn't appealing. Fortunately all the cops were at their favorite donut shops and twenty minutes later I was in my kitchen.

A bowl of Manhattan clam chopper and a cup of coffee did wonders. In no time I was back to normal. I started browsing though my wallet when I took out my insurance card. Expires December 17, it read. I glanced at the calendar. Today was the 16th! That meant I could ride another day. Now where would I ride to tomorrow? I wondered.